Self Love
Part 5
Embracing Authenticity

A Godly Life

LADY KIMBERLY MOTES DOTY

Awaken to You

The Path of Self Love and Acceptance

Part 5: Embracing Authenticity

Lady Kimberly Motes Doty

Self Love
Part 5

Embracing Authenticity

A Godly Life

Awaken to You: The Path of Self Love and Acceptance

Author: Lady Kimberly Motes Doty
Illustrator: Aurora Brand

ISBN 979-8-3481-6963-3 (Print ISBN paperback)

ISBN 979-8-3481-6970-1 (hardcover)

ISBN 979-8-3481-6964-0 (Ebook ISBN digital)

ISBN (audio)

Lady Kimberly Industries, LLC

15019 Madeira Way, 86174

Madeira Beach, Florida 33708-9998

LadyKimberlyIndustries.com

LadyKi.com

Amazon

https://www.amazon.com/author/ladykimberly

Lady Kimberly Books

https://mybook.to/LadyKimberlyBooks

Lady Kimberly Artwork & Photography

www.ArtPal.com/LadyKimberly

Table of Contents

Book Introduction

Welcome to a journey of self love, healing, and renewal—a transformative exploration designed to guide you toward a deeper understanding of yourself and the abundant life that awaits you. In a world often filled with chaos, expectations, and external pressures, it's easy to lose sight of our true selves. This book is an invitation to reconnect with your inner essence, embrace the beauty of who you are, and cultivate a profound sense of self acceptance.

Self love is not merely a buzzword; it is a fundamental aspect of our well-being and personal growth. It forms the foundation upon which we build our lives, influencing how we relate to ourselves and others. When we nurture self love, we create space for healing, allowing us to process past wounds and release the limiting beliefs that no longer serve us. This journey is about reclaiming your power, cultivating resilience, and discovering the joy that comes from living authentically.

Throughout this book, you will find practical tools, reflective exercises, and heartfelt anecdotes designed to support you in your quest for renewal. Each chapter delves into different facets of self love and healing, offering insights that encourage reflection and personal growth. You will explore the importance of setting healthy boundaries, the role of forgiveness in healing, and the transformative power of gratitude and mindfulness.

As you move through these pages, I encourage you to approach this journey with an open heart and a willingness to embrace vulnerability. Healing is not a linear process; it is a winding path filled with ups and downs, moments of clarity, and times of uncertainty. Be gentle with yourself as you navigate this terrain, recognizing that every step you take brings you closer to your true self.

This book is not just a guide; it is a companion on your journey. Together, we will explore the depths of self love, uncover the wisdom within, and celebrate the unique gifts that make you who you are. Remember, you are worthy of love, joy, and renewal, and this journey is yours to embrace.

So, let us embark on this adventure together, as we uncover the layers of self discovery, healing, and transformation that await.

Your path to self love and renewal begins now.

PROLOGUE

Self Love, Part 5, Embracing Authenticity
A Journey of Self Discovery and Connection

The gentle breeze brushes against my skin, carrying with it the refreshing scent of possibility and renewal. As I stand at the edge of the world, the vibrant colors of the setting sun blend into a breathtaking panorama, igniting a spark within me—a reminder of the beauty that life has to offer. In these serene moments, when I find solace in my own company, I feel an undeniable connection to something greater, a whisper of hope that resonates in my heart.

It is here, in the embrace of nature's tranquility, that I turn inward, exploring the depths of my mind and spirit. I seek a deeper understanding of my journey—a path filled with both challenges and gifts. This sacred space has witnessed my struggles, triumphs, and revelations, and it is from this wellspring of experience that I share the insights contained within this book.

These pages are not just a reflection of my personal journey; they represent a tapestry woven from the stories of many who have embarked on the quest for self love and healing. Each thread is infused with the wisdom gained from overcoming adversity and embracing vulnerability, highlighting the universal truth that we are all deserving of love, compassion, and renewal.

My intention in sharing this work is to walk alongside you as you navigate your own journey toward self discovery. Together, we will uncover the hidden treasures within, empowering you to embrace your true self and cultivate a life filled with love, joy, and authenticity. Our stories may be unique, but they share a common thread—a longing for healing, growth, and the fulfillment that comes from nurturing our inner selves.

As twilight descends and the first stars begin to twinkle in the night sky, I invite you to join me on this transformative journey. Let us delve into the wisdom that emerges when we quiet our minds and open our hearts, allowing us to rise above self doubt and limitations. Together, we will explore the infinite possibilities that await us on this path of self love and renewal.

There is so much healing, joy, and self discovery waiting for you. Embrace this adventure with an open heart, for your journey begins now.

~Lady Kimberly

Dedications

The Keys to My Journey

The completion of this book, as well as every word I have been able to share through my writing, is a testament to the unwavering support of the incredible individuals who have walked alongside me on this journey. As I reflect on the challenges I have faced—two battles with cancer and a lifelong struggle against RSD/CRPS—I am continually reminded of the profound power of faith and the compassion of those who have stood by my side.

To My Almighty Creator

With deep reverence and heartfelt gratitude, I dedicate "Radiant Reflections: Unleashing Beauty and Grace From Within" to You. Your divine wisdom has illuminated my path, granting me the strength to rise above every challenge. Through this book, I hope to share the knowledge and experiences that have shaped my journey, with the hope of inspiring others on their own quests for wholeness. May this work serve as a source of empowerment and light for all who read it. In Jesus Christ's holy name, Amen.

To My Beloved First Daughter

Diane, Your presence in my life has been a transformative gift, encouraging me to embrace the limitless potential within me. Your unwavering dedication and remarkable strength have shown me that no challenge is insurmountable. You embody beauty and grace, uplifting everyone fortunate enough to know you. This book is dedicated to you, my shining beacon of hope. May your light continue to inspire greatness in those around you, reminding them of their own strength. With all my love, Mom.

To My Beloved Baby Daughter

Tamara, you are a radiant symbol of strength and love, a guiding light through life's challenges. Your compassionate spirit touches the hearts of many, reflecting unwavering faith and kindness. I dedicate this book, "Optimal Wellness," to you, my precious Roo. Embrace life with positivity and grace, for you are a true blessing in this world.

To My Beloved Husband

Your love and unwavering strength have been my anchor during the most trying times. You believed in me when I could not see my own potential and encouraged me to rise above every obstacle. Your steadfast support has inspired me to embrace my own power and to face adversity with courage. This book is dedicated to you, my greatest source of inspiration. May it ignite the same flame in others, encouraging them to conquer their own mountains with love and self belief.

To My Precious Grandbabies

Braden, Aurora, Conor & Cade - You are my shining stars, illuminating my life with joy and wonder. The countless moments we've shared have woven beautiful memories into the fabric of my heart. Together, we've discovered the magic of the world and found beauty in life's simplest treasures. Our bond is unbreakable, transcending any distance. Let's continue to explore, learn, and create together, nurturing the flames of inspiration within us. You are my eternal source of love and joy. Keep shining bright, my little mermaid, mermen, and karate ninjas! I love you so much, my sweet grandbabies!

~Lady Kimberly

Acknowledgement

Tamara Brand

In this journey of self love and authenticity, I want to extend my heartfelt gratitude to my youngest daughter, Tamara, whose inspiring story serves as a radiant beacon of what it means to embrace oneself fully and unapologetically.

Tamara embodies the essence of living authentically, illustrating how self love can transform not only our lives but also the lives of those around us.

From her early years in high school, where she boldly celebrated her individuality through her passion for Ska music and distinct style, Tamara has consistently forged her own path, unafraid of societal norms or peer pressure. Her journey is a testament to strength of character and the power of self advocacy, particularly in the face of adversity.

The car accident that altered her physical capabilities could have easily defined her, yet she chose resilience. Instead of succumbing to limitations, Tamara turned her struggle into a profound lesson on compassion and self advocacy, sharing these insights with others and teaching her children the importance of openly communicating their needs.

As a supervisor and mentor, Tamara's empathy shines brightly. She fosters an environment of understanding and support, welcoming new team members with genuine care. Her commitment to modeling self love extends beyond her personal journey; she creates a workplace culture where every individual is valued, encouraging them to thrive in their unique ways.

Tamara's spirit of service is evident in her community engagement, whether rallying friends and family to assist after a hurricane or providing a safe haven for neighborhood children. Her home serves as a sanctuary—a warm, welcoming space where children find comfort, love, and understanding. The countless times I have witnessed her compassion, such as when she lovingly ensures that children are cozy and secure, highlights her incredible ability to create a nurturing environment.

Through her parenting, Tamara teaches emotional intelligence, guiding her children to recognize, express, and manage their feelings. This creates a home where vulnerability is celebrated, and deep connections are fostered. Her commitment to inclusivity and diversity enriches her social circles, encouraging meaningful conversations about identity and self acceptance.

Tamara's ongoing pursuit of personal growth and self care is an inspiration to us all. She understands that self love is a lifelong journey, and by prioritizing her well-being, she empowers herself to better serve her family and community. Her vision for a future filled with culture, creativity, and connection is a beautiful testament to her hope for a world where everyone looks out for one another, fostering genuine relationships that uplift us all.

Let Tamara's story encourage you to embrace your authenticity and cultivate self love. As my youngest daughter, she reminds me daily of the strength, resilience, and joy that comes from living true to oneself. Her example shows us that by honoring who we are and what we love, we can create lives filled with joy, fulfillment, and meaningful connections. The world needs more individuals like Tamara—those who dare to be different and inspire others to do the same. Thank you, Tamara, for your unwavering spirit and for being a source of light and inspiration in this journey toward self love and authentic living.

Chapter 7: The Importance Of Self Love In Today's World

Introduction

In a world that often feels overwhelming, where societal expectations and the relentless barrage of social media shape our Self perception, the importance of Self Love has never been more critical.

Societal Pressures to Conform

Every day, we are inundated with images and messages that tell us who we should be, what we should look like, and how we should live our lives. This constant pressure can lead to feelings of inadequacy, anxiety, and depression, creating a mental health crisis that affects millions. According to the World Health Organization, depression is now the leading cause of disability worldwide, impacting over 264 million people.

The Impact of Social Media on Self Perception

Social media amplifies these feelings, presenting curated snapshots of life that often leave us feeling inferior. The comparison trap can be particularly damaging, as we measure our worth against the highlight reels of others. Studies have shown that excessive social media use is linked to increased feelings of loneliness, envy, and dissatisfaction with one's life. The messages we consume can distort our Self image, leading us to believe that we are not enough.

Fostering Resilience Against Life's Challenges

Self Love serves as a powerful antidote to these challenges. It fosters resilience, allowing us to face life's hurdles with a sense of strength and purpose. Research indicates that individuals who practice Self Love are more equipped to manage stress, maintain healthy relationships, and embrace their true selves. In fact, a study published in the journal Self and Identity found that Self Compassion is strongly associated with emotional well-being and lower levels of anxiety and depression. When we cultivate a loving relationship with ourselves, we create a protective barrier against the negativity that can so easily seep in.

Imagine for a moment what your life would look like if you truly loved yourself. What if, instead of measuring your worth by external standards, you embraced your unique qualities and celebrated your individuality?

This question invites you to envision a reality where Self Acceptance is the foundation of your existence. Imagine waking up each day with a sense of gratitude for who you are, free from the comparisons and judgments that often cloud our minds.

Consider the impact this shift could have on your life. Self Love encourages us to prioritize our mental and emotional well-being, leading to healthier choices and a more fulfilling life. It empowers us to set boundaries, pursue our passions, and engage in relationships that uplift us. When we love ourselves, we begin to see the world through a lens of possibility rather than limitation.

As we embark on this journey together, remember that Self Love is not a destination but a continuous process of growth and discovery. It requires patience, practice, and compassion for ourselves. So, let's take the first step toward awakening to our true selves, embracing the power of Self Love to transform our lives and, in turn, the world around us.

Let this book be your guide as we explore the many facets of Self Love, unlocking the potential within you to live authentically and joyfully. Together, we will navigate the path of Self Acceptance, healing, and empowerment, creating a foundation for a brighter future.

To illustrate the transformative power of Self Love, let me share my daughter Tamara's personal journey with Self Love. -

Tamara's Personal Story
Embracing Authenticity & Self Love
Inspiring Journey of Tamara

Tamara embodies the essence of living authentically and with self love, serving as a radiant role model for us all. From a young age, she possessed remarkable clarity about who she was and an unwavering strength that propelled her to forge her own path, regardless of societal norms or peer pressure. While many of her high school friends were preoccupied with relationships and the latest fashion trends, Tamara passionately immersed herself in the vibrant world of Ska music, promoting bands and proudly sporting wide-leg jeans that celebrated her individuality.

Her journey of embracing authenticity and self love has been marked by resilience through adversity. Before she was a teen, Tamara was involved in a car accident that ruptured discs in her back, permanently affecting her physical health and ending her ability to play soccer—a sport she truly loved.

Despite facing ongoing neck and back pain, Tamara has learned to cope with her limitations, openly communicating her needs to her family and friends. This openness has nurtured a sense of understanding among her children and those around her, teaching them that everyone has different needs and sometimes requires space to heal.

Instead of letting this injury limit her, she transformed it into a powerful lesson on self advocacy and compassion that she shares with others.

In her professional life, Tamara has taken on a mentorship role, using her experiences to inspire those around her. As a supervisor, she understands that everyone has different learning styles and challenges. She has a natural ability to empathize with her team, welcoming new members with a warm smile and a genuine interest in their well-being. Her commitment to modeling self love extends beyond her own journey, as she fosters a supportive environment where everyone feels valued and understood.

Tamara's acts of service shines through her actions. During the recent hurricanes in Florida, she was the first neighbor to reach out, embodying kindness and community spirit. On the morning after the storm, she rallied her 9-year-old daughter, close friends, and neighbors to clean up debris, showing her selfless nature. Without hesitation, she selflessly helped with her downed tree limbs and then went to her neighbor's house, who worked long hours in healthcare, to assist with their yard.

Her home has become a sanctuary, a place for neighborhood children to seek comfort in her presence, where they feel welcome, understood, and loved, teaching them the importance of kindness and community. When parents need to run errands, the children often show up at Tamara's door, seeking comfort in her presence. Many times, I've walked into her home to find these children fast asleep on her couch, cocooned in cozy throws, while her own children quietly ensure they are comfortable. The peace they find in her home speaks volumes about the warmth and love that radiate from Tamara. She provides a safe haven, embodying a calm demeanor that assures them they are protected.

Through her parenting, Tamara practices emotional intelligence, guiding her children in recognizing and managing their own emotions. She encourages them to communicate their feelings openly, creating a home environment where vulnerability is celebrated rather than shamed. This ability to connect deeply with others has empowered her children to develop meaningful relationships and navigate their own emotional landscapes.

Tamara actively promotes inclusivity and diversity within her social circles. She has always been the first to greet anyone, regardless of their background, fostering a sense of belonging for all. Through thoughtful conversations about identity and self acceptance, she teaches her children the importance of embracing differences and understanding that everyone has a unique story.

Her personal growth and reflection are ongoing commitments. Tamara has learned to carve out time for herself amidst her busy life, engaging in activities like meditation, journaling, and simply unwinding with her children. She understands that self love is a lifelong journey and prioritizes her well-being to better serve her family and community.

Tamara's vision for the future is one filled with culture, creativity, and connection. She dreams of a neighborhood where people look out for one another not out of obligation but from a genuine desire to uplift each other. She envisions children playing safely in the streets while parents and grandparents share stories and laughter, fostering a sense of community that enriches everyone's lives.

Tamara's story encourages us all to live authentically, reminding us that self love is a powerful force that fuels our journey and the journeys of others. By embracing who we are and what we love, we create lives filled with joy, fulfillment, and genuine connections. Let Tamara's example inspire you to break free from societal expectations, honor your true self, and cultivate a life rich in self love and authenticity. The world needs more individuals like her—those who dare to be different and inspire others to do the same.

What To Expect From This Journey

Embarking on the journey of Self Love is a transformative experience, one that requires both commitment and openness. As you dive into this book, you will discover a structured path designed to guide you from understanding the core principles of Self Love to incorporating them into your daily life. Each part of this book unfolds like a roadmap, leading you through essential themes that will deepen your connection with yourself and empower you to embrace your unique journey.

Self Love, Part 1: Understanding Self Love: Understanding Self Love lays the groundwork for your exploration. Here, we will delve into the true meaning of Self Love, distinguishing it from Self Care and narcissism. You'll uncover the psychology behind Self worth and dispel common myths that may have hindered your progress. By understanding the foundation of Self Love, you will be equipped to recognize its vital role in your life.

Self Love, Part 2: The Journey Within: In the Journey Within, it invites you to embark on a personal exploration of your inner self. Through techniques aimed at Self discovery, you will engage with your emotions and thoughts, learning to accept your imperfections and identify your core values. This introspective journey is where the real magic happens, as you begin to cultivate a deeper understanding of who you are and what truly matters to you.

Self Love, Part 3: Practicing Self Love: Practicing Self Love provides practical tools and rituals to help you integrate Self Love into your daily life. You'll learn to create daily rituals that foster Self connection, craft personalized affirmations that uplift your spirit, and discover the profound connection between caring for your mind and body. These actionable steps will empower you to nurture yourself holistically, reinforcing the love you cultivate within.

Self Love, Part 4: Overcoming Obstacles: Overcoming Obstacles addresses the challenges that may arise on your journey. You'll explore strategies for conquering Self doubt, healing past wounds, and establishing healthy boundaries. By equipping yourself with these tools, you will be better prepared to navigate the obstacles that life may present, emerging stronger and more resilient.

Self Love, Part 5: Embracing Authenticity, in this book, you will discover how Self Love enhances your relationships, empowers you to advocate for yourself, and inspires others through your example. This part emphasizes that Self Love is not only a personal journey but also a powerful force for positive change in the world around you.

Self Love, Part 6: Nurturing Inner Beauty and Embracing Self Care: Nurturing Inner Beauty, Embracing Self Care cultivates in you the celebration of your journey. It delves into the essential practice of self care as a foundation for enhancing your inner beauty and overall well-being. You'll explore practical techniques for integrating self care into your daily routine, fostering mindfulness, creativity, and connection with nature. This book emphasizes the importance of self acceptance and self compassion while encouraging you to build supportive relationships that uplift your journey. By prioritizing self care, you empower yourself to nurture your unique qualities and cultivate a life filled with confidence and radiance.

Self Love, Part 7: The Freedom of Healthy Boundaries" is a transformative guide that explores the vital connection between self love and the establishment of healthy boundaries in various aspects of life. Through insightful discussions and practical exercises, this book empowers you to recognize your intrinsic worth, embrace your uniqueness, and cultivate a compassionate relationship with yourself. It delves into different types of boundaries—emotional, physical, digital, and more—highlighting their importance in fostering mutual respect and understanding in relationships. As you embark on this journey of self discovery, you learn to navigate societal pressures, overcome obstacles, and prioritize your well-being, ultimately unlocking the potential for a fulfilling and authentic life grounded in love, resilience, and empowerment. As you progress through the chapters, I encourage you to keep a journal. Use it to capture your thoughts, feelings, and insights as you navigate this journey. Reflecting on your experiences will deepen your understanding and reinforce the lessons you learn along the way.

Setting intentions for what you hope to achieve is also essential. Take a moment to pause and consider: What do you wish to gain from this journey? Whether it's increased confidence, healthier relationships, or a greater sense of peace, articulating your goals will help you stay focused and motivated.

Remember, this journey of Self Love is uniquely yours. Embrace it with an open heart and a willingness to explore. Together, we will uncover the beauty of Self Acceptance and the transformative power of loving yourself wholeheartedly. Let's embark on this journey together, step by step, toward a life filled with love, joy, and authenticity.

How To Use This Book For Transformation
Living a Life of Self Love in Relationships

Welcome to your journey of Self Love, particularly as it pertains to relationships! This book serves as more than just a collection of insights; it is an interactive guide designed to facilitate your personal growth and transformation in the context of your connections with others. It invites you to engage deeply with the material, encouraging you to reflect, practice, and embody the principles of Self Love within your relationships.

As you move through each chapter, remember that this is a personal journey, not a race. Take your time to absorb the information, allowing the concepts to resonate and integrate into your life. Each section builds upon the last, creating a comprehensive framework for understanding and implementing Self Love in your relationships. Approach this journey with an open heart and a willingness to reflect on your experiences and interactions.

Reflection is a powerful tool for transformation, particularly in relationships. At the end of each chapter, you will find exercises and prompts that encourage you to pause and consider how the material relates to your connections with others. These reflective practices are designed to help you internalize the lessons and apply them to your unique circumstances. Embrace this opportunity to explore your thoughts, feelings, and beliefs about Self Love in relationships, and allow yourself the space to grow.

To kickstart your journey, take a moment to consider your current challenges related to Self Love in your relationships. What thoughts or beliefs have held you back from fostering deeper connections? Perhaps you struggle with setting boundaries, expressing your needs, or overcoming feelings of inadequacy. Write down these challenges in your journal, allowing yourself to be honest and open. This exercise will serve as a foundation for your journey, providing clarity on areas where you seek growth and healing.

As you progress through the book, revisit these reflections periodically. After completing each section, take a moment to assess how your perspective has shifted. Are the challenges you noted still as prominent? Have you gained new insights or strategies to address them? Tracking your progress will illuminate your growth and reinforce your commitment to embracing Self Love within your relationships.

Transformation is a journey, not a destination. It requires patience, practice, and an unwavering belief in your worth. By engaging with this book as an interactive guide and allowing yourself the time and space to reflect, you will unlock the potential for profound change in your life and relationships.

Together, let's embark on this transformative journey, nurturing the seeds of Self Love and acceptance within you. Each step you take brings you closer to the authentic, empowered version of yourself that you are meant to be. Embrace the process, and remember that every moment spent in self reflection is a step toward cultivating healthier, more fulfilling connections with those around you.

Visualization Exercise
Embracing Self Love in Relationships

Get Comfortable

Take a moment to get comfortable. Find a quiet space where you won't be disturbed, and allow yourself to settle into a relaxed position.

Close Your Eyes

Close your eyes gently.

Begin to Take Slow Deep Breathes

Begin to take a series of deep breaths—inhale deeply through your nose, allowing your abdomen to rise, and then exhale slowly through your mouth, releasing any tension you might be holding. With each breath, feel yourself becoming more present, more grounded in this moment.

Imagine Waking Up in the Morning

Now, as you continue to breathe deeply, I invite you to imagine waking up in the morning. Picture the first rays of sunlight gently streaming through your window, illuminating your room with a warm, golden glow. Feel the softness of your sheets against your skin as you stretch and awaken. This is a new day, a fresh start filled with possibilities.

Imagine Looking in the Mirror With Confidence & Contentment

Visualize yourself opening your eyes, and instead of feelings of anxiety or self doubt, you are met with a profound sense of confidence and contentment. Imagine looking in the mirror and seeing not just your reflection, but a person who embodies love, strength, and authenticity. Allow yourself to feel the warmth of self acceptance washing over you, affirming that you are enough just as you are.

As You Imagine Stepping Out of Bed, Think About Embracing Self Love

Now, as you step out of bed, think about how embracing self love will influence your interactions with others throughout the day. Visualize yourself moving through your morning routine with intention, knowing that your well-being is your priority.

Imagine Which Relationships to Nurture with Self Love

Picture the relationships you will nurture today. Imagine engaging with loved ones, friends, or colleagues. Feel the difference in your interactions when you approach them from a place of self love. You communicate openly and honestly, expressing your needs and boundaries with kindness and confidence.

Imagine the Joy of Sharing Laughter, Support

Visualize the joy of sharing laughter, support, and encouragement, knowing that these connections are built on mutual respect and understanding.

Imagine the Self Love Positive Energy that Flows Between You & Those You Care About

As you continue to envision your interactions, imagine the positive energy that flows between you and those you care about. Picture how self love enhances your ability to listen and empathize, creating deeper connections. You are not just giving love; you are also receiving it, allowing it to fill your heart and soul. Feel the warmth of these loving relationships, knowing that they reflect the love and acceptance you have for yourself.

Think About the Dreams You Would Pursue If Self Love Guided You

Next, consider the dreams you would pursue if self love guided your choices in relationships. Visualize the goals you have longed to achieve—the passions you've put on hold due to fear or doubt. Picture yourself sharing these aspirations with your loved ones, feeling their support and encouragement as you take steps toward those dreams. Whether it's starting a new creative project, pursuing a career change, or dedicating time to a hobby that brings you joy, embrace the belief that you are worthy of pursuing what sets your soul on fire.

Reflect How it Feels to Live with Self Love as Your Guide

As you continue to visualize this empowered version of yourself, take a moment to reflect on how it feels to live with self love as your guiding principle in your relationships.

Notice the Lightness in Your Heart

Notice the lightness in your heart, the clarity in your mind, and the sense of peace that envelops you. Allow this feeling to expand, filling every corner of your being with warmth and positivity.

When Ready, Bring Your Awareness Back to Present

When you're ready, gently begin to bring your awareness back to the present moment. Wiggle your fingers and toes, feeling the surface beneath you.

Take One Last Deep Breath, Inhaling Love & Confidence

Take one last deep breath, inhaling the love and confidence you've cultivated, and exhale any remaining doubts or fears.

As You Open Your Eyes, Carry This Sense of Self Love With You Today

As you open your eyes, carry this sense of self love into your interactions today. Remind yourself that you have the power to create loving, fulfilling relationships that honor your true self. Each step toward self love enhances your ability to connect authentically with others. You are deserving of all the love and joy the world has to offer, and this journey begins with you.

Statistics & Research On Self Love & Mental Health In Relationships

In the context of relationships, self love plays a crucial role in fostering healthy connections and enhancing overall well-being. Here are updated statistics and research findings that specifically address self love as it relates to relationships, underscoring its importance in living a life of self love.

Mental Health Benefits in Relationships

Research published in the Journal of Social and Personal Relationships indicates that individuals who practice self love experience improved emotional health within their relationships. They report lower levels of relationship anxiety and are better equipped to handle conflicts. This emotional stability allows them to engage more positively with their partners, reducing the likelihood of toxic dynamics.

Resilience & Relationship Coping

A study from the University of California, Berkeley, highlights that self love contributes to resilience not just personally, but also within relationships. Participants who exhibit self acceptance demonstrate a greater capacity to navigate relational challenges, such as miscommunication or disagreements, effectively bouncing back from conflicts and strengthening their bonds.

Healthier Relationship Dynamics

According to research in the Journal of Happiness Studies, individuals who cultivate self love are more likely to establish and maintain healthy boundaries in their relationships. This leads to enhanced empathy, compassion, and open communication, resulting in more supportive and nurturing partnerships. Those who love themselves are less likely to tolerate unhealthy behaviors, which contributes to more fulfilling relationships.

Positive Impact on Self Esteem & Relationships

A meta-analysis in the Journal of Personality and Social Psychology found that self love is closely linked to self esteem, which directly influences relationship satisfaction. Individuals who view themselves positively tend to attract and foster healthier relationships, as they are less dependent on external validation and more confident in their interactions.

Social Media, Self Perception, & Relationships

A 2020 study from the Royal Society for Public Health revealed that social media impacts self esteem and relationship perceptions. Users who engage in positive self talk and practice self love are more resilient against comparison and negative influences from social media, which allows them to maintain healthier relationships both online and offline.

Mindfulness & Relationship Quality

Research published in Psychological Science shows that mindfulness enhances self love, which translates to better emotional regulation in relationships. Individuals who are mindful and self loving are more adept at managing their emotions during relational stressors, leading to improved conflict resolution and overall relationship satisfaction.

Long-Term Relationship Health Outcomes

A longitudinal study from the University of Michigan indicates that self compassion contributes to healthier long-term relationship outcomes.

Couples who practice self love and acceptance are less likely to engage in destructive behaviors, such as criticism or withdrawal, and more likely to support each other's growth and well-being.

These findings emphasize the transformative power of self love, especially in the context of relationships. By prioritizing self acceptance and compassion, individuals can enhance their mental health, build resilience, and foster healthier connections with others. Embracing self love is essential not only for personal growth but also for creating and maintaining fulfilling relationships, allowing both individuals and partnerships to thrive.

Reflective Questions

1. What does self love mean to me personally?

   Take a moment to define self love in your own words.

____

____

____

How do you envision it manifesting in your life? ___________

____

____

____

2. How do societal expectations and pressures affect my self perception? _______________________________

____

____

____

Reflect on the messages you've internalized from society. In what ways do these expectations influence how you view yourself?

____

____

____

____

3. In what situations do I find myself comparing my life to others on social media? _______________________________

____

____

Identify specific instances where social media has triggered feelings of inadequacy or envy. How did these experiences impact your self esteem?

____

____

____

4. What are some ways I can foster resilience against negative influences in my life? _______________________________

____

____

Consider strategies or practices that you can implement to build a stronger sense of self worth and resilience.

____

____

____

____

____

5. How do I currently practice self compassion in my daily life? ____

____

____

Reflect on your self talk and how you respond to your own mistakes or shortcomings. Are there areas where you can be more compassionate toward yourself?

____

____

____

6. What beliefs or narratives about myself do I need to challenge or let go of? ____________________________________

____

____

Identify any limiting beliefs that have held you back. What steps can you take to reframe these narratives in a more positive light? ______________________________________

____

____

____

____

7. How would my life change if I fully embraced self love?

____

____

____

Imagine the possibilities that could unfold if you prioritized self love. What specific changes do you envision in your relationships, career, or personal well-being? ______________

____

____

____

____

8. What are my unique qualities and strengths that I can celebrate? ____

____

____

Take time to acknowledge your individuality. What aspects of yourself do you appreciate and want to embrace more fully?

____

____

____

____

9. How can I create a daily practice that nurtures my self love?

____

____

____

____

____

____

____

Consider rituals or activities that resonate with you, such as journaling, meditation, or affirmations. How can you incorporate these into your routine? _______________________

____

____

____

____

____

____

____

____

____

10. What goals do I hope to achieve on this journey of self love and acceptance? ____

____

____

____

____

____

____

Reflect on your intentions for this journey. What specific outcomes do you wish to achieve as you cultivate a deeper relationship with yourself? _______________________________

____

____

____

____

____

____

By engaging with these reflective questions, you can deepen your understanding of the concepts discussed in the chapter and begin to apply them to your own lives. This process of self reflection can serve as a powerful catalyst for growth and transformation as you embark on your journey of self love.

Chapter 1: Self Love, Part 1, Understanding Self Love

Why It's Important To Begin With Self Love, Part 1, Understanding Self Love

Part 1: Understanding Self Love serves as the essential foundation for the entire journey of self discovery and personal growth outlined in this book series.

In a world filled with external pressures and rapid changes, self love is a fundamental concept that anchors our emotional and mental well-being.

This part of the book introduces the profound practice of valuing and accepting oneself wholeheartedly, recognizing intrinsic worth, embracing uniqueness, and treating oneself with kindness and compassion.

Understanding Self Love

Understanding self love is not merely a starting point; it is the rich soil in which all other aspects of personal growth are rooted. Just as a garden requires nurturing to flourish, so does your relationship with yourself. Without a solid foundation of self love, any attempts at self improvement or healing may feel shallow or ineffective. This part lays the groundwork for genuine transformation, helping you build a nurturing relationship with yourself that supports emotional resilience and authentic living.

Key Concepts Explored

1. What Is Self Love?

Self love is the practice of valuing and accepting yourself wholeheartedly. It involves recognizing your intrinsic worth, embracing your uniqueness, and treating yourself with kindness and compassion. This book sets the stage for understanding the profound importance of self love as the cornerstone of emotional and mental well-being. We explore the key pillars of Self Love, each offering unique insights and practices to help nurture a deeper connection with ourselves and foster a more fulfilling life:

1. Self Acceptance
2. Self Worth
3. Authenticity
4. Setting Healthy Boundaries
5. Self Compassion
6. Releasing Negative Self Talk
7. Mindfulness
8. Self Care
9. Servitude

2. True Self Love vs. Self Care & Narcissism

Self love is distinguished from self care and narcissism, emphasizing that self love is the deeper belief that we deserve acts of care. Self love is the nurturing soil that makes self care meaningful, while narcissism is an excessive focus on yourself that often leads to insecurity and a lack of empathy. Understanding these distinctions helps you cultivate a healthy and balanced relationship with yourself.

3. The Role of Self Love in Upholding Morals

Self love is essential for maintaining personal values and integrity. It empowers us to cultivate self confidence and resilience, enabling us to uphold our morals in the face of life's challenges.

4. The Journey of Self Love

Self love is a continuous process that requires patience and dedication. Understanding Self Love encourages you to approach the journey with an open heart and a willingness to embrace vulnerability, recognizing that healing and self discovery are not linear but a winding path filled with ups and downs.

5. Historical Context & Theories of Self Love

The concept of self love has evolved over centuries, influenced by cultural, philosophical, and psychological perspectives. This chapter provides a historical overview, highlighting the significance of self love in promoting mental health and emotional well-being.

6. Embracing Imperfections

Accepting imperfection is a liberating experience that allows you to let go of unrealistic expectations and embrace your authentic self. Understanding Self Love explores the power of embracing flaws and shares stories of individuals who have transformed their perceived shortcomings into sources of strength and inspiration.

7. Identifying Core Values

We begin identifying and understanding your core values in Part 1, which is essential for enhancing self love. This book guides you through exercises to reflect on significant moments in your life, create a values list, prioritize your values, and visualize your ideal life. Aligning your actions with your core values fosters a deeper sense of purpose and fulfillment.

The Journey Ahead

By beginning with Self Love, Part 1, Understanding Self Love, you set the stage for a transformative experience that will unfold throughout the entire series. Each subsequent part builds upon the foundational understanding of self love, guiding you through deeper exploration, emotional healing, and personal empowerment. This journey is uniquely yours, and by embracing each step with patience, compassion, and an open heart, you pave the way for a more fulfilling and authentic life. Each Part or Book, builds upon the foundational

understanding of self love, guiding you through self discovery, emotional healing, and personal empowerment.

Reading and Reflecting through the entire series will provide you with a comprehensive roadmap to self love and wellbeing, empowering you to thrive despite the challenges you face. Let this journey be your guide to a life filled with love, joy, and renewal. Your path to self love and renewal begins now.

By beginning with Self Love, Part 1, Understanding Self Love, you set the stage for a transformative experience that will unfold throughout the entire series. This foundation of self love will enable you to:

- Cultivate a richer, more fulfilling life by honoring your true self.

- Build resilience and navigate life's challenges with greater ease.

- Foster healthier relationships grounded in empathy and compassion.

- Align your actions with your core values, leading to authentic living.

Each book in the series is designed to deepen your understanding and practice of self love, offering practical tools, reflective exercises, and heartfelt anecdotes. As you progress through the series, you will uncover layers of self discovery, healing, and transformation, ultimately leading to a more fulfilling and joyful life.

Your Path Forward

As you continue your journey through the series, embrace each part, each book, as a stepping stone towards greater self awareness and personal growth. The time to love yourself is now—take that first step with Self Love, Part 1: Understanding Self Love, continue with Self Love, Part 2: The Journey Within, and Self Love, Part 3: Practicing Self Love, Self Love, Part 4: Overcoming Obstacles, Self Love, Part 5: Living a Life of Self Love and conclude with Self Love, Part 6: Nurturing Inner Beauty and Embracing Self, and watch how it transforms your world, guiding you towards a life of authenticity, purpose, and profound self acceptance.

Read Self Love, Part 7, The Freedom of Healthy Boundaries, anytime after you feel you have a positive understanding of Self Love, Part 1, Understanding Self Love.

Reading through the entire series will provide you with a comprehensive roadmap to self love and well-being, empowering you to thrive despite the challenges you face. Let this journey be your guide to a life filled with love, joy, and renewal.

Watch how this book series and your work transforms your world, guiding you towards a life of authenticity, purpose, and profound self acceptance.

Let this journey be your guide to a life filled with love, joy, and renewal!

Chapter 2: Self Love, Part 2, The Journey Within

In Self Love, Part 2, The Journey Within, the focus shifts to the transformative process of self discovery, guiding you on an introspective journey to uncover you inner selves. This chapter emphasizes that understanding oneself is not merely a destination but a continuous exploration of thoughts, emotions, and beliefs that shape our identities.

Discovering Your Inner Self

The book opens by highlighting the profound nature of self discovery, inviting you to delve into various self exploration techniques. These tools—including journaling, meditation, guided imagery, and mindfulness practices—serve to enhance self awareness and emotional intelligence.

Each technique is accompanied by practical exercises designed to help you articulate you feelings and understand the intricate connections between thoughts and emotions.

Self Exploration Techniques

Journaling

Encourages free expression of thoughts and feelings, offering a safe space for reflection and growth tracking.

Guided Imagery

Utilizes visualization to explore desires and fears, fostering a deeper connection with aspirations.

Meditation

Promotes mindfulness and presence, enabling individuals to connect with their inner selves by observing their thoughts and emotions without attachment.

Mindfulness Practices

Cultivates present-moment awareness, enhancing self acceptance and attunement to one's inner self.

Identifying Emotions & Thought Patterns

You are guided to recognize you emotions and thought patterns through exercises like emotional check-ins, thought records, and the use of a feelings wheel. These practices not only enhance emotional vocabulary but also empower you to understand how you feelings influence you behaviors and relationships.

Emotional Intelligence

The chapter emphasizes the significance of emotional intelligence, a skill set encompassing self awareness, self regulation, motivation, empathy, and social skills. By cultivating emotional awareness, we can make informed decisions that align with our core values, thereby enhancing our overall well-being.

Accepting Imperfection

In the subsequent chapter, you are reminded of the power of embracing your flaws as integral to authenticity. Accepting imperfection serves as a pathway to personal growth and resilience, allowing you to connect with others on a deeper level and foster a culture of acceptance.

Identifying Core Values

The journey continues with an exploration of core values, which serve as guiding principles in life. Recognizing and aligning actions with core values enhances Self Love and authenticity. The chapter guides you through reflective exercises to identify and prioritize your values, ultimately leading to a more fulfilling and purposeful life.

Conclusion: the Journey Within

The Journey Within is a call to action for you to engage in the lifelong process of self discovery. It emphasizes that understanding oneself is not just about finding answers but

about asking the right questions and embracing the complexities of one's inner world. By cultivating self awareness, emotional intelligence, and a commitment to personal values, you can navigate life's challenges with resilience and authenticity.

As you conclude this part of the series, you are inspired to continue your journey within, unlocking the potential for growth and fulfillment that lies in embracing your true selves.

Your Path Forward

As you continue your journey through the series, embrace each part, each book, as a stepping stone towards greater self awareness and personal growth. The time to love yourself is now—take that first step with Self Love, Part 1, Understanding Self Love, continue with Self Love, Part 2, The Journey Within, and Self Love, Part 3, Practicing Self Love, Self Love, Part 4, Overcoming Obstacles, Self Love, Part 5, Living a Life of Self Love and conclude with Self Love, Part 6, Nurturing Inner Beauty and Embracing Self, and watch how it transforms your world, guiding you towards a life of authenticity, purpose, and profound self acceptance.

Read Self Love, Part 7, The Freedom of Healthy Boundaries, anytime after you feel you have a positive understanding of Self Love, Part 1, Understanding Self Love.

Reading through the entire series will provide you with a comprehensive roadmap to self love and well-being, empowering you to thrive despite the challenges you face. Let

this journey be your guide to a life filled with love, joy, and renewal.

Watch how this book series and your work transforms your world, guiding you towards a life of authenticity, purpose, and profound self acceptance.

Let this journey be your guide to a life filled with love, joy, and renewal!

Self Love, Part 3, Practicing Self Love

Introduction

Self Love, Part 3, Practicing Self Love is a comprehensive guide designed to help readers integrate self love into their daily lives through practical tools, rituals, and insights.

The book emphasizes the importance of self acceptance, caring for both mind and body, and establishing healthy boundaries as foundational elements of self love.

By fostering self connection and encouraging readers to embrace their unique qualities, the book provides a pathway to a more fulfilling and authentic life.

Key Components

Practical Tools & Rituals

The book includes a variety of actionable steps, such as daily rituals for self connection, personalized affirmations, and mindfulness practices, all aimed at integrating self love into everyday routines.

Fostering Self Acceptance

It emphasizes the significance of self acceptance, encouraging readers to embrace their imperfections and recognize their intrinsic worth.

Daily Rituals for Self Connection

Readers learn how to create mindful morning and evening routines that promote reflection, gratitude, and self care.

Crafting Personal Affirmations

The book guides readers in developing personalized affirmations that uplift their spirits and reinforce positive self perception.

Mind-Body Connection

It explores the profound connection between caring for one's mind and body, highlighting the importance of nutrition, exercise, and sleep in maintaining overall well-being.

Holistic Nurturing

The book encourages a holistic approach to self love, suggesting practices that nurture emotional, physical, and spiritual health.

Establishing Healthy Boundaries

It discusses the importance of setting and maintaining healthy boundaries as a vital aspect of self love, providing practical strategies for effective communication.

Creative Expression

The chapter on creative expression emphasizes its role in self discovery and emotional healing, encouraging readers to explore various forms of creativity.

Connecting With Nature

The book highlights the benefits of spending time in nature as a means of nurturing mental and emotional well-being.

Conclusion: Embrace Your Self Love Journey

Self Love, Part 3, Practicing Self Love successfully delivers on its promise to provide practical tools and insights for integrating self love into daily life. The book not only covers the essential components listed but also expands on the theme of self love by exploring creative expression and nature connection, making it a well-rounded resource for personal growth. Readers are encouraged to embrace the journey of self love, fostering a deeper understanding of themselves and their unique paths. Overall, this book serves as a powerful guide for anyone seeking to cultivate a more loving and fulfilling relationship with themselves.

As you embark on this journey, remember that Self Love is not merely a destination—it's a continuous practice that empowers you to live authentically and vibrantly. Embrace these rituals and affirmations as vital components of your personal growth, allowing them to illuminate your path toward a more fulfilling and empowered existence.

With the insights and practices from Self Love, Part 3, you'll be inspired to take actionable steps in your Self Love journey, nurturing your inner garden and allowing it to flourish. Don't miss the opportunity to dive deeper into these transformative practices by exploring Part 3, Practicing Self Love for a more enriched and empowered life!

Your Path Forward

As you continue your journey through the series, embrace each part, each book, as a stepping stone towards greater self awareness and personal growth. The time to love yourself is now—take that first step with Self Love, Part 1, Understanding Self Love, continue with Self Love, Part 2, The Journey Within, and Self Love, Part 3, Practicing Self Love, Self Love, Part 4, Overcoming Obstacles, Self Love, Part 5, Living a Life of Self Love and conclude with Self Love, Part 6, Nurturing Inner Beauty and Embracing Self, and watch how it transforms your world, guiding you towards a life of authenticity, purpose, and profound self acceptance.

Read Self Love, Part 7, The Freedom of Healthy Boundaries, anytime after you feel you have a positive understanding of Self Love, Part 1, Understanding Self Love.

Reading through the entire series will provide you with a comprehensive roadmap to self love and well-being, empowering you to thrive despite the challenges you face. Let this journey be your guide to a life filled with love, joy, and renewal.

Watch how this book series and your work transforms your world, guiding you towards a life of authenticity, purpose, and profound self acceptance.

Let this journey be your guide to a life filled with love, joy, and renewal!

Self Love, Part 4, Overcoming Obstacles

Introduction

Self Love, Part 4, Overcoming Obstacles is an empowering exploration of the challenges that can hinder our journey toward Self Love and personal growth. This section focuses on two significant themes: conquering self doubt and healing from past wounds, providing you with practical strategies to navigate your emotional landscape and cultivate resilience.

Conquering Self Doubt

Self doubt is a formidable adversary that can undermine confidence and stifle ambition. This chapter delves into effective strategies for managing negative thoughts and fostering a more empowered mindset. You will learn to recognize and acknowledge your self doubt, challenge negative thoughts, and reframe your inner dialogue.

Key Strategies Include

Practicing Self Compassion

Treating oneself with kindness and understanding, especially during moments of uncertainty.

Keeping a Journal

Documenting instances of self doubt and reflections on overcoming them to build clarity and resilience.

Visualization Techniques

Employing mental imagery to picture success and reinforce positive beliefs.

Building Resilience Against Criticism

Developing a growth mindset that views challenges and feedback as opportunities for personal development.

This chapter empowers you to dismantle the barriers of self doubt, encouraging you to embrace your authentic self with confidence.

Healing Wounds From The Past

The journey toward Self Love necessitates confronting and healing from past wounds. In this chapter, you are guided through the process of acknowledging past experiences, allowing yourself to feel associated emotions, and ultimately reframing your narratives.

Key elements of healing include:

Forgiveness

Understanding forgiveness as a transformative act that releases emotional burdens and fosters freedom.

Processing Emotions

Engaging in self reflection to identify how past experiences shape current beliefs and behaviors.

Moving Forward

Emphasizing that forgiveness is an ongoing journey that requires patience and self compassion.

By addressing past wounds, you can cultivate a healthier relationship with yourself, paving the way for deeper self acceptance and emotional well-being.

Establishing Healthy Boundaries

Setting healthy boundaries is essential for nurturing Self Love and fostering meaningful relationships. This chapter explores the importance of boundaries, providing practical guidance on how to set and communicate them effectively.

Key topics include:

Understanding the Need for Boundaries

Recognizing how boundaries protect emotional health and promote respect in relationships.

Practical Steps for Boundary-Setting

Reflecting on personal needs, identifying specific boundaries, practicing assertive communication, and maintaining consistency.

Common Challenges

Addressing obstacles such as guilt, fear of conflict, and past experiences that may hinder boundary-setting efforts.

This chapter empowers you to assert your needs confidently, leading to healthier relationships and a stronger sense of self worth.

Conclusion: Embrace Your Journey

Self Love, Part 4, Overcoming Obstacles serves as a vital resource for anyone seeking to navigate the challenges of self doubt, past wounds, and boundary-setting. By implementing the strategies outlined in this section, you are equipped to confront your obstacles head-on, fostering resilience and emotional healing.

As you embark on this journey of overcoming obstacles, remember that you are not alone. Each challenge presents an opportunity for growth and transformation. Embrace the process, and allow the insights from this part of the series to inspire you to pursue your dreams with confidence and authenticity.

Don't miss the chance to dive deeper into these essential topics by exploring Part 4, Overcoming Obstacles. Embrace your potential for Self Love and personal empowerment today!

Your Path Forward

As you continue your journey through the series, embrace each part, each book, as a stepping stone towards greater self awareness and personal growth. The time to love yourself is now—take that first step with Self Love, Part 1, Understanding Self Love, continue with Self Love, Part 2, The Journey Within, and Self Love, Part 3, Practicing Self Love, Self Love, Part 4, Overcoming Obstacles, Self Love, Part 5, Living a Life of Self Love and conclude with Self Love, Part 6, Nurturing Inner Beauty and Embracing Self, and watch how it

transforms your world, guiding you towards a life of authenticity, purpose, and profound self acceptance.

Read Self Love, Part 7, The Freedom of Healthy Boundaries, anytime after you feel you have a positive understanding of Self Love, Part 1, Understanding Self Love.

Reading through the entire series will provide you with a comprehensive roadmap to self love and well-being, empowering you to thrive despite the challenges you face. Let this journey be your guide to a life filled with love, joy, and renewal.

Watch how this book series and your work transforms your world, guiding you towards a life of authenticity, purpose, and profound self acceptance.

Let this journey be your guide to a life filled with love, joy, and renewal!

Chapter 5: Self Love, Part 5, Embracing Authenticity

Self Love In Relationships

Self Love is not just an individual journey; it profoundly influences our relationships with others. When we cultivate a loving and compassionate relationship with ourselves, it enhances our ability to connect authentically with those around us. This chapter will explore how Self Love enhances our connections and provide insights into nurturing healthy relationships.

How Self Love Enhances Your Connections

At its core, Self Love is about recognizing and embracing our worth. When we truly love ourselves, we create a solid foundation for our interactions with others.

Here are several ways Self Love enhances our connections:

Improved Communication

Self Love fosters clarity in our thoughts and feelings, enabling us to communicate more effectively. When we value ourselves, we are more likely to express our needs, desires, and boundaries openly. This honest communication helps prevent misunderstandings and builds stronger connections.

Healthy Boundaries

Self Love empowers us to establish and maintain healthy boundaries. When we value our time, energy, and emotional well-being, we are more likely to communicate our limits to others. Healthy boundaries create a safe space for mutual respect and understanding, allowing relationships to flourish without resentment or overextension.

Increased Empathy & Compassion

Loving ourselves allows us to extend that love and compassion to others. When we practice Self Acceptance, we become more empathetic toward the struggles and challenges faced by those around us. This empathy deepens our connections and fosters a sense of understanding and support within our relationships.

Reduced Dependence on Others

When we cultivate Self Love, we develop a sense of independence that allows us to rely on ourselves for validation and happiness. This reduces the pressure on our relationships to fulfill all our emotional needs. Instead, we engage with others from a place of abundance rather than lack, leading to more balanced and fulfilling connections.

Enhanced Resilience in Conflict

Every relationship encounters challenges and conflicts. When we practice Self Love, we build resilience that allows us to navigate these difficulties with grace. We are less likely to take things personally and more capable of finding constructive solutions. This resilience fosters a sense of security and trust in our relationships.

Increased Authenticity

Self Love encourages us to embrace our true selves, flaws and all. When we accept ourselves, we become more authentic in our interactions. This authenticity attracts genuine connections and allows us to build relationships based on honesty and vulnerability.

Nurturing Healthy Relationships

While Self Love lays the groundwork for healthy connections, nurturing those relationships requires intentional effort and care. Here are some practical strategies to foster healthy relationships infused with Self Love:

Prioritize Communication

Make open and honest communication a priority in your relationships. Regularly check in with your loved ones, sharing your thoughts and feelings while also encouraging them to do the same.

Practicing active listening—being fully present and engaged when others speak—can strengthen your connections and foster a deeper understanding of one another.

Practice Gratitude

Cultivating an attitude of gratitude can enhance your relationships. Regularly express appreciation for the people in your life and acknowledge the positive impact they have on you. Simple gestures, such as sending a thank-you note or verbally expressing your gratitude, can strengthen bonds and create a positive atmosphere.

Engage in Shared Activities

Spend quality time engaging in activities that you enjoy together. Shared experiences create memories and foster a sense of connection. Whether it's cooking, hiking, or simply watching a movie, finding common interests helps deepen your bond and keeps the relationship vibrant.

Encourage Individual Growth

Support one another's personal growth and aspirations. Encourage your loved ones to pursue their passions and interests, just as you should for yourself. Celebrate each other's accomplishments, no matter how small, and create an environment where growth is nurtured and embraced.

Address Conflicts With Compassion

Conflict is inevitable in any relationship, but how we address it matters. Approach conflicts with compassion and a willingness to understand the other person's perspective. Use "I" statements to express your feelings and avoid placing blame. For example, "I feel hurt when..." instead of "You always make me feel..." This approach fosters empathy and helps resolve conflicts constructively.

Set Boundaries Together

Establishing boundaries is not only a personal endeavor but also a collective one. Discuss and agree on boundaries that work for both parties in the relationship. This may include time spent together versus alone time, communication preferences, or how to navigate challenging situations. Setting boundaries together promotes mutual respect and understanding.

Foster a Supportive Environment

Create an environment where both individuals feel safe to express themselves without judgment. Encourage open dialogue about feelings, challenges, and dreams. A supportive environment fosters trust and intimacy, allowing the relationship to thrive.

Self Love & Relationships Reciprocal Nature

As we delve into the profound relationship between self love and the connections we cultivate in our lives, it's important to recognize the reciprocal nature of this dynamic. Self love and healthy relationships exist in a symbiotic relationship, where nurturing one can enhance and strengthen the other.

When we embark on the journey of self love, we lay the foundation for cultivating meaningful, fulfilling relationships. By recognizing our inherent worth and embracing our authentic selves, we create a solid internal framework that allows us to engage with others from a place of confidence, clarity, and emotional resilience. This self assurance empowers us to communicate our needs, set healthy boundaries, and approach conflict with compassion - all of which contribute to the development of strong, supportive connections.

Authentic Relationships Deepen Self Love & Acceptance

Conversely, being in relationships that are built on mutual respect, understanding, and emotional safety can also deepen our self love and self acceptance. Surrounding ourselves with individuals who see our worth, celebrate our strengths, and offer unconditional support reinforces the positive beliefs we hold about ourselves. When we experience the transformative power of being truly seen and accepted by others, it can profoundly impact our relationship with ourselves.

The Reciprocal Dynamic

This reciprocal dynamic is akin to a garden, where self love is the fertile soil and our relationships are the vibrant blooms that thrive within it. As we nurture the self love within, we create the optimal conditions for our connections to flourish. And as those connections grow stronger and more nourishing, they, in turn, feed back into our self love, creating a continuous cycle of personal growth and relational fulfillment.

It's important to recognize that this reciprocal relationship is not a one-way street. While self love lays the groundwork for healthy relationships, the relationships we cultivate can also become a powerful source of self love and self acceptance. When we engage with others who mirror our inherent worth and support our personal evolution, it reinforces the belief that we are worthy of love, belonging, and authentic connection.

The interplay between self love and healthy relationships is a profound and multifaceted dynamic. As we continue to explore this reciprocal relationship, it's essential to understand the deeper layers of how they influence and enhance one another.

When we cultivate a strong foundation of self love, we become more attuned to our needs, boundaries, and values. This clarity allows us to attract and engage in relationships that are truly aligned with our authentic selves. We are less likely to compromise our well-being or settle for connections that do not serve our highest good. Instead, we are empowered to seek out and nurture relationships that uplift us, challenge us to grow, and provide a safe space for vulnerability and emotional intimacy.

Conversely, being in relationships that foster mutual understanding, respect, and support can have a profound impact on our self love. As we experience the transformative power of being seen, heard, and accepted for who we are, it reinforces the belief that we are worthy of such care and connection. The mirroring we receive from our loved ones can help us recognize and celebrate the inherent beauty and strengths that we may have overlooked or diminished within ourselves.

The act of supporting one another's personal growth and celebrating each other's triumphs can deepen the self love we hold. When we witness the people in our lives thriving and fulfilling their potential, it inspires us to do the same. We are motivated to continue our own journey of self discovery and self acceptance, knowing that we have a network of individuals who will champion our efforts and uplift us along the way.

It's important to note that this reciprocal relationship is not limited to romantic partnerships or familial bonds. Friendships, mentorships, and even community connections can also play a vital role in nurturing our self love. When we surround ourselves with a diverse network of individuals who embody self compassion and encourage our growth, it creates a supportive ecosystem that amplifies our own self love.

As we deepen our understanding of this reciprocal dynamic, we begin to recognize that self love and healthy relationships are not separate entities, but rather intertwined aspects of a fulfilling and purposeful life. By cultivating self love, we create the foundation for cultivating relationships that reflect and reinforce our inherent worth. And by engaging in relationships that are rooted in mutual respect, empathy, and support, we further nourish and expand the self love that resides within us.

This reciprocal dance is a lifelong journey, one that requires patience, self awareness, and a willingness to be vulnerable. But the rewards of this harmonious interplay are immense – a life filled with genuine connections, emotional fulfillment, and a deep, unshakable sense of self love that radiates outward, touching the lives of all those around us.

By embracing the reciprocal nature of self love and relationships, we empower ourselves to create a life that is rich in both personal fulfillment and meaningful, nourishing connections. As we continue our journey of self love, we must remember that the relationships we build can serve as a reflection of the love we have cultivated within, while also contributing to the ongoing expansion of that self love.

Navigating Relationship Challenges With Self Love

Relationships, no matter how meaningful and fulfilling, will inevitably encounter challenges, conflicts, and disappointments along the way. In these moments, it is essential to approach these difficulties from a place of self love, rather than self criticism or despair. By cultivating self love as the foundation for navigating relational challenges, we empower ourselves to respond with wisdom, compassion, and resilience.

Guidance on Approaching Relationship Difficulties

When faced with relationship challenges, it's important to resist the urge to immediately blame yourself or your partner. Instead, take a step back and approach the situation with a compassionate, self loving mindset. Reflect on the core needs and values that are at the heart of the conflict, and seek to understand the perspectives of all involved.

Rather than jumping to conclusions or making assumptions, approach the situation with genuine curiosity and a willingness to find a constructive solution. Communicate your thoughts and feelings openly, using "I" statements to express your experience without placing undue judgment on others. Remember that every person in the relationship is on a journey of growth, and temporary setbacks do not negate the inherent worth and humanity of any individual.

Strategies for Maintaining Self Compassion

It's natural to feel hurt, frustrated, or disappointed when facing relational difficulties. However, it's crucial that we avoid slipping into a cycle of self criticism or self blame. Self compassion is the antidote to this harmful pattern, allowing us to approach the challenge with kindness, understanding, and a commitment to our own well-being.

When emotions run high, take a moment to pause and reflect. Remind yourself that you are doing the best you can, and that the current situation does not define your worth or the value of the relationship. Engage in self soothing practices, such as deep breathing, journaling, or spending time in nature, to calm your mind and reconnect with your inner strength.

Additionally, be mindful of the self talk you engage in. Replace harsh, judgmental thoughts with compassionate, encouraging statements. Imagine how you would comfort a dear friend facing a similar challenge, and extend that same level of care and understanding to yourself.

How Self Love Empowers Us

Self love is the foundation that empowers us to navigate relationship challenges in a healthy, constructive manner. When we deeply value ourselves, we are more equipped to set clear boundaries, communicate our needs effectively, and approach conflict resolution with a spirit of mutual respect and understanding.

Self love grants us the courage to have difficult conversations, to assert our needs, and to walk away from situations that are no longer serving us. It allows us to take responsibility for our own emotions and actions, while also extending grace and empathy to our partners. With self love as our guide, we can engage in the messy work of relationship repair and growth, knowing that our inherent worth remains intact, regardless of the outcome.

Self love cultivates the emotional resilience needed to weather the storms of relational challenges. When we can hold ourselves with compassion, we are less likely to become overwhelmed or paralyzed by the difficulties we face. Instead, we can draw upon our inner reserves of strength, creativity, and perseverance to navigate a path forward that honors the needs of all involved.

By embracing self love as the foundation for navigating relationship challenges, we empower ourselves to build connections that are authentic, fulfilling, and growth-promoting. We learn to communicate our boundaries with clarity, resolve conflicts with empathy, and emerge from adversity with a renewed sense of self worth and purpose. This self love, in turn, strengthens our ability to create and sustain healthy, nourishing relationships throughout our lives.

Letting Go With Self Love

Relationships, whether romantic, familial, or platonic, have the power to profoundly impact our lives. However, there may come a time when we must make the difficult decision to release an unhealthy relationship or let go of an attachment that is no longer serving our highest good. In these moments, the role of self love becomes paramount, providing the courage, clarity, and self compassion needed to navigate this transformative process.

Importance of Self Love in Releasing Unhealthy Relationships

Cultivating a deep well of self love is essential when it comes to letting go of relationships that have become toxic, draining, or no longer align with our values and aspirations. Without a strong foundation of self worth and self acceptance, it can be tempting to cling to unhealthy connections out of fear, habit, or a misguided belief that we are undeserving of something better.

Self love empowers us to recognize the signs of an unhealthy relationship and muster the courage to make the necessary changes. It allows us to see ourselves as worthy of respect, kindness, and genuine connection – qualities that may have been lacking in the relationship we are now releasing. By tapping into our self love, we can detach from the emotional hold these unhealthy bonds may have had on us, making space for more nourishing relationships to enter our lives.

Self Love's Courage & Clarity To End What Is No Longer Serving Us

When we cultivate self love, we gain the clarity and courage to end relationships that are no longer serving our highest good. This clarity allows us to discern when a connection has become stagnant, abusive, or simply outgrown its purpose in our lives. With self love as our guide, we can make the difficult yet necessary decision to let go, even when it may be painful or uncomfortable in the short term.

The courage that self love instills empowers us to have honest conversations, set firm boundaries, and ultimately walk away from relationships that deplete our energy, undermine our well-being, or prevent us from growing into our fullest selves. This courage is not born of brashness or callousness, but rather a deep understanding that we deserve to surround ourselves with people who uplift, support, and challenge us in healthy ways.

The Role of Self Compassion in the Grieving Process

Ending a relationship, even one that has become unhealthy, can be a profoundly difficult and emotional experience. As we navigate the grieving process, self compassion becomes a vital ally in our healing journey.

Self compassion allows us to acknowledge the pain, disappointment, and sense of loss that may arise, without judging or berating ourselves for these natural human emotions. It encourages us to treat ourselves with the same kindness and understanding we would extend to a dear friend going through a similar experience.

By practicing self compassion, we create a safe space to fully feel and process our emotions, rather than suppressing or numbing them. This, in turn, enables us to move through the grief with greater ease, allowing us to eventually find closure, acceptance, and the freedom to open ourselves to new, healthier connections.

Ultimately, the role of self love in the process of letting go cannot be overstated. It provides us with the clarity to discern when a relationship has run its course, the courage to make the necessary changes, and the self compassion to tenderly navigate the emotional aftermath. By embracing self love as our guiding light, we empower ourselves to release what no longer serves us, making way for relationships that are truly nourishing, fulfilling, and aligned with our highest selves.

Modeling Self Love For Others

As we cultivate self love within ourselves, we begin to radiate an energy that can have a profound and positive influence on the relationships in our lives.

By embodying self acceptance, self compassion, and a deep reverence for our own worth, we can inspire and uplift those around us to embark on their own journeys of self love.

Self Love's Positive Inspiration & Influence on Relationships

When we make the courageous choice to prioritize self love, it sends a powerful message to our loved ones, friends, and community. Our willingness to honor our needs, set healthy boundaries, and treat ourselves with kindness serves as a beacon, illuminating the path for others to do the same.

As we navigate our relationships from a place of self love, we model for others what it looks like to engage authentically, communicate openly, and resolve conflicts constructively.

Our ability to advocate for ourselves, while also extending empathy and understanding, creates an environment that fosters mutual respect and growth.

Ripple Effect

Self love can have a ripple effect, inspiring those around us to reflect on their own self worth and the quality of their connections. When others witness the joy, confidence, and fulfillment that radiates from us, it can ignite a desire within them to embark on their own journey of self discovery and self acceptance.

Your Self Acceptance as a Living Example

By being a living example of self love and self acceptance, we encourage others to cultivate these qualities within themselves. Our very presence, our willingness to be vulnerable, and our commitment to our own growth can serve as a powerful catalyst for change in the lives of those we hold dear.

When we unapologetically embrace our unique strengths, quirks, and imperfections, we send a message that self acceptance is not only possible but also profoundly liberating. By sharing our stories of overcoming challenges, facing our fears, and learning to love ourselves, we create space for others to feel seen, heard, and inspired to do the same.

Setting Healthy Boundaries & Prioritizing Self Care & Advocating for our Needs

By setting healthy boundaries, prioritizing self care, and advocating for our needs, we demonstrate that self love is not a selfish act, but rather a necessary foundation for living a fulfilling and purposeful life. This living example can empower our loved ones to follow suit, empowering them to honor their own needs and cultivate the self love they deserve.

How to Model Healthy Behaviors

As we strive to be a positive influence on the relationships around us, it's important to consistently model healthy behaviors that reflect our self love. Here are some ways we can do so:

Establish & Communicate Clear Boundaries

Be transparent about your needs, limits, and preferences, and hold firm to these boundaries with grace and compassion.

Prioritize Self Care Practices

Engage in activities that nourish your mind, body, and spirit, and share the benefits of these practices with your loved ones.

Advocate for Your Needs & Desires

Speak up for yourself, express your ideas, and celebrate your accomplishments, encouraging others to do the same.

Approach Conflicts and Challenges With Empathy & Problem-Solving

Model how to navigate difficulties in a constructive manner, focusing on mutual understanding and growth.

Express Gratitude & Appreciation

Regularly acknowledge the positive impact others have on your life, fostering an environment of mutual support and validation.

By consistently embodying these self love-infused behaviors, we create a ripple effect that can transform the relationships in our lives. Our loved ones will witness the joy, confidence, and fulfillment that radiates from us, inspiring them to cultivate self love in their own unique ways.

Ultimately, the power of modeling self love lies in its ability to inspire, empower, and uplift those around us. As we continue on our journey of self acceptance, we have the opportunity to be a beacon of hope, courage, and authentic connection, guiding our loved ones towards a more fulfilling and purposeful life.

Interdependence Vs. Co-Dependency

As we deepen our understanding of self love and its role in our relationships, it's crucial to distinguish between the healthy, mutually supportive dynamic of interdependence and the detrimental patterns of codependency. By cultivating self love, we empower ourselves to engage in interdependent relationships that enrich our lives, while avoiding the pitfalls of unhealthy attachments.

Distinguishing Interdependent & Codependent Relationships

Interdependent Relationships

Codependent Relationships

Healthy Balance of Autonomy & Connection

Interdependent relationships are characterized by a healthy balance of autonomy and connection. In these partnerships, individuals maintain a strong sense of self while also supporting and relying on one another. There is a mutual exchange of care, respect, and understanding, with each person's needs and boundaries being honored.

Unhealthy Emotional & Phycological Reliance

In contrast, codependent relationships are marked by an unhealthy emotional and psychological reliance on the other person. Codependency often arises from a lack of self love, where individuals seek to derive their self worth and identity from the relationship, rather than from within. This can lead to a loss of personal boundaries, constant need for validation, and an inability to function independently.

How Self Love Empowers Interdependent Relationships

When we cultivate self love, we create the foundation for engaging in interdependent relationships that enrich our lives without compromising our sense of self. Self love grants us the confidence to be vulnerable, the clarity to communicate our needs, and the resilience to navigate challenges alongside our loved ones.

Self Love Empowers Equality in Relationships

With a strong sense of self worth, we are able to approach our relationships as equals, contributing to the partnership while also maintaining our individuality. We recognize that our worth is not contingent on the approval or validation of others, allowing us to form connections that are genuine, supportive, and empowering.

Setting Healthy Boundaries Ensures our Needs Are Met

Self love empowers us to set healthy boundaries, ensuring that our needs are met without becoming overly dependent on our partners. We can ask for support when needed, while also respecting the autonomy and boundaries of those close to us. This balance fosters an environment of mutual respect, trust, and personal growth.

Recognizing & Avoiding Codependent Patterns

Recognizing the signs of codependency is an essential step in cultivating healthy, self love-infused relationships. Some common indicators of codependency include:

- ▸ Difficulty making decisions without the input or approval of your partner

- ▸ Feeling incomplete or lost without the other person

- ▸ Sacrificing your own needs and boundaries to please your partner

- ▸ Experiencing intense emotional turmoil or a sense of crisis when the relationship is disrupted

- ▸ Difficulty expressing your own thoughts, feelings, and desires

Codependency is a deeply ingrained and often insidious pattern that can have a profoundly negative impact on our relationships and overall well-being.

Signs Of Codependency

It is essential to develop a keen awareness of the signs of codependency, as recognizing these patterns is the first step towards breaking free and cultivating healthier, more fulfilling connections.

Difficulty in Making Decisions

One of the hallmarks of codependency is the difficulty in making decisions without constant input or approval from a partner. Codependent individuals often feel incapable of trusting their own judgment or making choices that do not align with their partner's preferences. This reliance on external validation can stem from a deep-seated belief that their own thoughts and opinions are not valid or worthy.

Feeling of Being Incomplete or Lost

Closely related to this is the feeling of being incomplete or lost without the presence of the other person. Codependent partners may experience a profound sense of emptiness, anxiety, or even panic when separated from their significant other, as they have come to rely on the relationship as the primary source of their identity and self worth. This can lead to a complete loss of personal autonomy and a blurring of individual boundaries.

Sacrificing Your Own Needs

Another common sign of codependency is the tendency to sacrifice one's own needs and boundaries in order to please a partner. Codependent individuals often find it challenging to assert their needs, fears, or desires, instead choosing to prioritize the needs of their partner at the expense of their own well-being. This pattern can manifest in a variety of ways, such as agreeing to things they are uncomfortable with, neglecting self care, or constantly putting the partner's agenda first.

Intense Emotional Turmoil When Relationship Disrupted

Codependent relationships are often characterized by a heightened emotional reactivity and a sense of crisis when the relationship is disrupted in any way. The prospect of the relationship ending, or even experiencing a minor conflict, can trigger intense feelings of abandonment, anxiety, or even despair. This emotional volatility can make it exceedingly difficult for codependent partners to navigate challenges in a healthy, constructive manner.

Difficulty Expressing Your Own Thoughts, Feelings & Desires

Lastly, codependency can also manifest as a profound difficulty in expressing one's own thoughts, feelings, and desires. Codependent individuals may have become so accustomed to suppressing their authentic selves in order to maintain the relationship that they lose touch with their inner voice and personal boundaries. This can lead to a profound sense of disconnection from oneself and an inability to advocate for one's needs.

If you recognize these codependent patterns in your own relationships, it is crucial to take proactive steps to address them. This may involve engaging in individual therapy, where you can explore the root causes of your codependency and develop strategies for building a stronger, more resilient sense of self. Additionally, setting clear boundaries, both within the relationship and in your own life, can be a powerful tool for reclaiming your autonomy and personal agency.

Ultimately, the journey of overcoming codependency is deeply intertwined with the cultivation of self love. By nurturing a deep appreciation and acceptance for who you are, independent of any relationship, you empower yourself to engage in healthier, more fulfilling connections that enrich your life rather than define it. It is a challenging process, but one that holds the promise of greater personal growth, authentic intimacy, and the freedom to live a life that is truly your own.

By embracing self love, we empower ourselves to break free from codependent dynamics and instead nurture interdependent relationships that allow for personal growth, mutual support, and a deep sense of fulfillment. This journey requires ongoing self reflection and a willingness to prioritize our own well-being, but the rewards are immense – relationships that truly enrich and elevate our lives.

Nurturing Self Love In Relationships

While the journey of self love is inherently personal, the relationships we cultivate can play a vital role in supporting and enhancing this transformative process. By engaging in practices that foster self love, both individually and collectively, we can create an environment that uplifts, empowers, and celebrates the unique worth of each person involved.

Cultivating Self Love in Relationships

There are a variety of practices and exercises that couples, friends, or any close-knit group can explore together to nurture self love within the relationship dynamic.

Engage in Regular Affirmation Exchanges

One powerful practice is to engage in regular affirmation exchanges. Set aside time to share positive affirmations about each other, highlighting the unique strengths, qualities, and accomplishments that you admire. This not only reinforces the self love of the recipient but also encourages the person offering the affirmation to recognize and celebrate their own worth.

Self Love "Vision Board"

Another collaborative exercise is to create a "self love vision board" together. Gather images, words, and symbols that represent self acceptance, self care, and the embodiment of each person's authentic self. This shared activity can foster deeper understanding, inspire personal growth, and create a tangible reminder of the self love you are cultivating as a group.

Practicing Gratitude

Practicing gratitude is another invaluable tool for nurturing self love within relationships. Take turns expressing appreciation for one another, acknowledging the ways in which your loved ones have supported, uplifted, and empowered your self love journey. This exchange of gratitude can deepen the bond between you while also reinforcing the inherent worth of each individual.

Supporting Each Other's Journey

As you and your loved ones navigate the path of self love, offering unwavering support for each other's personal growth can strengthen the relationship bond in profound ways. By championing each other's self love journeys, you create an environment of mutual encouragement, empathy, and accountability.

Celebrate the Victories

When one person in the relationship experiences a breakthrough or overcomes a challenge related to self love, celebrate that victory together. Acknowledge the courage, resilience, and self compassion that was required, and let your loved one know that you are honored to witness their transformation. This shared sense of accomplishment can inspire you all to continue cultivating self love with even greater dedication.

Be Compassionate & Understanding

Conversely, when someone is struggling with self doubt or self criticism, respond with compassion and understanding. Offer a listening ear, validate their feelings, and remind them of their inherent worth. Avoid judgment or attempts to "fix" the situation, as this can undermine the self love you are collectively nurturing. Instead, focus on providing a safe, supportive space for your loved one to process their emotions and rediscover their inner strength.

Importance of Individual Self Worth

While cultivating self love within the context of relationships is invaluable, it's crucial to maintain an environment that celebrates and uplifts the individual self worth of each person involved. Avoid comparisons, competition, or any dynamic that could undermine the self love of one partner or friend.

Create Safe Spaces

Create a space where everyone feels seen, heard, and accepted for who they are. Encourage open communication about personal boundaries, needs, and growth areas, and respect each person's unique journey. By fostering an atmosphere of mutual respect and unconditional acceptance, you empower one another to deepen your self love without fear of judgment or rejection.

Self Love Is Not a Zero Sum Game

Remember, the self love you nurture within your relationships is not a zero-sum game. As each person grows in self acceptance and self worth, the entire group benefits from the collective radiance and empowerment. This synergistic effect can transform your relationships into a tapestry of support, inspiration, and celebration of the unique brilliance that each individual brings to the table.

Embrace Holistically Approach

Embracing this holistic approach to nurturing self love within your relationships is a testament to the power of connection, collaboration, and the belief that we are all deserving of love - both from ourselves and from those who matter most to us.

Self Love In Relationships Conclusion

As we conclude our exploration of self love in relationships, it's clear that the interplay between these two profound aspects of our lives is a reciprocal and deeply transformative dance. By cultivating a strong foundation of self love, we create the optimal conditions for nurturing healthy, fulfilling relationships.

Our self acceptance, self compassion, and commitment to our own well-being empower us to communicate our needs, set boundaries, and engage with others from a place of authenticity and mutual respect. This, in turn, attracts connections that mirror and reinforce our inherent worth, further nourishing the self love we hold within.

Conversely, being in relationships that foster mutual understanding, support, and celebration can have a profound impact on our self love. As we experience the transformative power of being seen, heard, and accepted for who we are, it reinforces the belief that we are worthy of such care and connection. The mirroring we receive from our loved ones can help us recognize and celebrate the unique strengths and qualities that we may have previously overlooked or diminished.

This reciprocal dynamic is not limited to romantic partnerships or familial bonds. Friendships, mentorships, and even community connections can all play a vital role in nurturing our self love and enriching the relationships we cultivate. When we surround ourselves with a diverse network of individuals who embody self compassion and encourage our growth, it creates a supportive ecosystem that amplifies our own self love.

As we navigate the inevitable challenges and conflicts that arise within our relationships, it is essential that we approach these difficulties from a place of self love. By maintaining self compassion, clear communication, and a commitment to mutual understanding, we empower ourselves to resolve conflicts constructively and emerge from adversity with an even stronger sense of self worth and relational fulfillment.

The role of self love becomes paramount when we must make the difficult decision to release an unhealthy relationship or let go of an attachment that is no longer serving our highest good. In these moments, self love provides us with the clarity, courage, and self compassion needed to navigate this transformative process, allowing us to create space for more nourishing connections to enter our lives.

Ultimately, the reciprocal nature of self love and relationships is a profound testament to the interconnectedness of our personal growth and our ability to cultivate meaningful, fulfilling connections. By embracing this synergistic dynamic, we empower ourselves to live lives that are rich in both self acceptance and genuine, supportive relationships - a harmonious tapestry that uplifts our spirits, expands our perspectives, and inspires us to continue on our journey of self discovery and relational fulfillment.

As we move forward, may we continue to nurture the self love that resides within, knowing that it will continue to shape and enhance the quality of the relationships we cultivate. And may we, in turn, allow those relationships to further deepen and strengthen the self love that serves as the foundation for a life filled with authenticity, joy, and profound connection.

Chapter 6: Becoming Your Own Champion

Becoming your own champion is a vital aspect of Self Love and personal empowerment. It means standing up for yourself, advocating for your needs, and confidently expressing your thoughts and feelings. Self advocacy is essential in various areas of life, from personal relationships to professional environments. In this chapter, we will explore the importance of Self advocacy and provide techniques for assertive communication that can help you become your own champion.

Becoming Your Own Champion

Becoming your own champion is a vital aspect of Self Love and personal empowerment. It means standing up for yourself, advocating for your needs, and confidently expressing your thoughts and feelings. Self advocacy is essential in various areas of life, from personal relationships to professional environments. In this chapter, we will explore the importance of Self advocacy and provide techniques for assertive communication that can help you become your own champion.

Importance of Self Advocacy

Self advocacy is the ability to represent and defend your own interests and needs. It is rooted in Self Awareness, Self Respect, and the belief that you deserve to have your voice heard. Here are several reasons why Self advocacy is crucial:

Empowerment

Advocating for yourself empowers you to take control of your life and decisions. It reinforces the belief that you have the right to express your needs and desires. This empowerment fosters a sense of agency, allowing you to navigate challenges with confidence and resilience.

Improved Relationships

Self advocacy plays a crucial role in building healthy relationships. When you express your needs and boundaries clearly, you create an environment of openness and honesty. This transparency fosters mutual respect and understanding, enhancing the quality of your connections.

Enhanced Self Worth

When you advocate for yourself, you reinforce your Self worth and value. Acknowledging your needs and standing up for them sends a powerful message to yourself and others: you deserve respect and consideration. This affirmation contributes to a healthier Self image and a deeper sense of Self Love.

Increased Opportunities

In professional settings, Self advocacy can lead to greater opportunities for growth and advancement. By confidently expressing your ideas, skills, and accomplishments, you position yourself as a valuable contributor. This proactive approach can open doors to new possibilities and career advancements.

Conflict Resolution

Self advocacy equips you with the tools to navigate conflicts effectively. When you can articulate your feelings and needs, you are better prepared to address disagreements constructively. This ability to communicate assertively fosters healthier resolutions and prevents misunderstandings.

Techniques For Assertive Communication

Assertive communication is a key component of Self advocacy. It involves expressing your thoughts, feelings, and needs in a clear and respectful manner while also respecting the rights and feelings of others. Here are some techniques to help you communicate assertively:

Use "I" Statements

Frame your thoughts and feelings using "I" statements to express your perspective without sounding accusatory. For example, instead of saying, "You never listen to me," try, "I feel unheard when I try to share my ideas." This approach focuses on your experience and reduces the likelihood of defensiveness from others.

Be Clear & Specific

When communicating your needs or feelings, be clear and specific. Vague statements can lead to misunderstandings. Instead of saying, "I need more support," you might say, "I would appreciate it if we could set aside time each week to discuss our projects together." Specificity helps ensure your message is understood.

Calm & Confident Tone

Your tone of voice significantly impacts how your message is received. Aim to speak calmly and confidently, avoiding a tone that is aggressive or passive. Practicing a steady tone helps convey assertiveness and allows you to express your needs without escalating tensions.

Practice Active Listening

Assertive communication is a two-way street. Practice active listening by giving your full attention to the other person when they speak. Show that you value their perspective by nodding, maintaining eye contact, and paraphrasing what they say to ensure understanding. This approach fosters respectful dialogue and strengthens relationships.

Set Boundaries Clearly

When advocating for yourself, be clear about your boundaries. State what is acceptable and what is not in a direct and respectful manner. For instance, if someone frequently interrupts you, you can say, "I appreciate your input, but I would like to finish my thought before we discuss it further." Clear boundaries help reinforce your needs.

Be Open to Feedback

While advocating for yourself, remain open to feedback from others. This openness demonstrates a willingness to engage in constructive dialogue and fosters mutual respect. Listen to their perspective and consider their input while still standing firm in your own beliefs and needs.

Practice Assertiveness in Low-Stakes Situations

If you find assertive communication challenging, start practicing in low-stakes situations. This could involve expressing your preferences in casual conversations, such as where to eat or what movie to watch. Gradually building your assertiveness in these smaller contexts can help you feel more confident in higher-stakes situations.

Visualize Successful Outcomes

Before entering a conversation where you need to advocate for yourself, take a moment to visualize a successful outcome. Imagine yourself communicating confidently and effectively. This mental rehearsal can help reduce anxiety and reinforce your belief in your ability to advocate for yourself.

Becoming Your Own Champion Conclusion

Becoming your own champion through Self advocacy is a powerful expression of Self Love and empowerment. By standing up for your needs and communicating assertively, you create a life that reflects your values and desires. Remember that advocating for yourself is not selfish; it is an essential aspect of honoring your worth and fostering healthy relationships.

As you practice Self advocacy and assertive communication, be patient with yourself. This journey may require time and effort, but each step you take toward becoming your own champion reinforces your Self Love and confidence.

Embrace your voice, affirm your needs, and celebrate the empowerment that comes with advocating for yourself. In doing so, you pave the way for a more fulfilling and authentic life.

Empowerment: Heart Of Self Advocacy

When you engage in self advocacy, you take an active role in shaping your life and decisions. This sense of empowerment is a crucial aspect of self love and personal growth. By standing up for your needs and expressing your desires, you reinforce the belief that you have the inherent right to do so. This agency allows you to navigate challenges with greater confidence and resilience, seeing yourself as the primary driver of your life's direction.

Recognizing Your Worth

You Value Yourself: Advocating for yourself demonstrates that you value your own well-being and are willing to take the necessary steps to ensure your needs are met. This proactive approach fosters a feeling of control over your life, rather than passively accepting circumstances or relying solely on others to meet your needs. As you consistently advocate for yourself, you cultivate an internal locus of control, recognizing yourself as the primary agent responsible for your life's outcomes. This recognition is fundamental in developing a strong sense of self worth and confidence.

Aligning Actions With Values

Solutions That Reflect Your Authentic Self : This empowerment extends to how you approach problem-solving and decision-making. When you advocate for yourself, you are more likely to explore solutions that align with your values and priorities, rather than compromising or deferring to the preferences of others. This self directed mindset allows you to make choices that genuinely reflect your authentic self, leading to a greater sense of fulfillment and alignment in your life. By staying true to your values, you create a life that resonates with who you are at your core.

Commanding Respect

You Deserve to Be Heard & Acknowledged : The act of self advocacy sends a powerful message to both yourself and others about your worth and capabilities. By standing up for your needs, you demonstrate that you believe you deserve to be heard, respected, and accommodated. This self assurance can have a transformative effect on your self image, reinforcing the idea that you are worthy of having your voice and desires recognized. Remember, your opinions and needs matter, and asserting them is a vital part of your journey toward empowerment.

Cultivating Resilience

The Courage to Prioritize Your Well-Being: As you continue to advocate for yourself, you may encounter resistance or pushback from others. However, navigating these challenges with resilience and determination further strengthens your sense of empowerment. Each time you assert your needs and boundaries, you prove to yourself that you have the courage and conviction to prioritize your well-being, even in the face of adversity. Embrace these moments as opportunities for growth, as each challenge you overcome builds your strength and reinforces your commitment to self care.

Additional Reflection: Empowerment In Action

Empowerment is not just a concept; it is an action and a mindset. It involves continuously advocating for yourself in various aspects of your life—be it in personal relationships, professional settings, or your own self care practices. The more you practice self advocacy, the more natural it becomes, and the stronger your sense of empowerment will grow.

Set Clear Intentions

Begin each day by setting intentions that reflect your values and goals. This practice can guide your actions and decisions, ensuring that you remain aligned with your authentic self.

Celebrate Your Wins

Acknowledge and celebrate your achievements, no matter how small. Each step you take toward self advocacy and empowerment is a victory worth recognizing.

Engage in Community

Surround yourself with like-minded individuals who support and uplift your journey. Community can provide encouragement and reinforce the importance of self advocacy.

By embracing empowerment through self advocacy, you not only enhance your own life but also inspire others to do the same. Together, we can create a culture that values authenticity, respect, and mutual support. May this section encourage you to take bold steps toward living your truth and advocating for your needs, leading to a fulfilling and empowered life.

Enhanced Self Worth: The Power Of Self Advocacy

When you advocate for yourself, you are actively affirming your self worth and intrinsic value. Acknowledging your needs and standing up for them sends a powerful message to both yourself and others: you believe you deserve respect, consideration, and the fulfillment of your desires. This act of self advocacy is a vital component of self love, and it plays a significant role in shaping your self image.

Affirming Your Value

Self advocacy reinforces the core belief that you are worthy of having your voice heard and your preferences honored. When you refuse to silence or diminish yourself, you demonstrate a profound respect and appreciation for who you are. This self affirmation can have a lasting impact on your self image, helping to counteract any feelings of inadequacy or unworthiness that may have previously held you back.

By making a conscious decision to advocate for your needs, you declare that your feelings, desires, and boundaries are valid and important. This acknowledgment serves as a powerful reminder that you are deserving of love, understanding, and fulfillment. Each time you stand up for yourself, you reinforce this belief, creating a positive feedback loop that strengthens your sense of self worth over time.

Healing Wounds of Insecurity

As you advocate for yourself, you are essentially signaling to both yourself and the world that you are a person of inherent value. You deserve to have your unique desires, perspectives, and experiences recognized and validated. This powerful message can help heal any wounds or insecurities you may have carried regarding your self worth.

Every time you assert your needs, you are actively working to dismantle the negative narratives that may have taken root in your mind. You are challenging the beliefs that say you are not enough or that your needs are unimportant. In this way, self advocacy becomes a form of self therapy, allowing you to reclaim your narrative and reshape your self perception.

Modeling Self Respect for Others

When you advocate for yourself, you are modeling self respect and self love for those around you. By standing up for yourself, you set an example that inspires others to do the same. This can create a ripple effect, contributing to a culture of mutual respect and empowerment within your relationships and communities.

When others witness your commitment to self advocacy, they are more likely to reflect on their own relationships with self worth. Your actions can inspire friends, family, and colleagues to advocate for their own needs and desires, fostering an environment where everyone feels empowered to express their authentic selves. This collective empowerment can lead to healthier, more supportive relationships, where all individuals feel valued and respected.

Self Advocacy as Self Care

It's important to note that self advocacy is not about being selfish or narcissistic. Rather, it is an act of self care and self compassion. By honoring your needs and boundaries, you create the conditions for a more authentic, fulfilling, and balanced life.

When you prioritize your well-being, you also enable yourself to show up more fully and generously in your relationships and other areas of your life. You become less likely to experience burnout or resentment because you have taken the time to acknowledge and address your own needs. In doing so, you create a healthier dynamic where you can give and receive love more freely.

Practical Steps To Enhance Your Self Worth Through Advocacy

Identify Your Needs

Take time to clarify what you truly need in various areas of your life—emotionally, physically, and mentally. Write them down and reflect on their importance.

Practice Assertiveness

Use "I" statements to express your feelings and needs. For example, "I feel overwhelmed when my boundaries are not respected, and I need more support."

Set Boundaries

Clearly define what is acceptable for you in your relationships and communicate these boundaries to others. Remember, boundaries are an essential part of self respect.

Celebrate Your Progress

Acknowledge the small victories along the way. Each instance of self advocacy is a step toward greater self worth and authenticity.

Seek Support

Surround yourself with people who respect your self advocacy efforts. Share your journey with friends or groups who encourage mutual empowerment.

By embracing self advocacy, you embark on a transformative journey that enhances your self worth and empowers you to live more authentically. Remember, you are deserving of respect, consideration, and the fulfillment of your desires. As you continue to advocate for yourself, you not only strengthen your own self image but also inspire those around you to embrace their worthiness as well.

Improved Relationships: The Transformative Power Of Self Advocacy

Self advocacy plays a crucial role in building and maintaining healthy, fulfilling relationships. When you express your needs, boundaries, and preferences clearly, you create an environment of openness, transparency, and mutual respect. This foundational shift not only enhances the quality of your interactions but also fosters deeper connections with those around you.

Establishing Openness & Transparency

By advocating for yourself, you signal to others that your voice and experiences matter. This sets the stage for more authentic and equitable connections, where each person's needs are acknowledged and honored. Instead of suppressing or minimizing your desires to please others, self advocacy empowers you to engage in relationships as your true, unapologetic self.

This authenticity invites others to reciprocate, encouraging them to share their own needs and feelings. As both parties express themselves openly, the relationship deepens, leading to a more profound understanding of one another. This exchange of vulnerability cultivates trust, paving the way for a supportive and enriching partnership.

Reducing Misunderstandings & Resentment

The act of self advocacy fosters an atmosphere of trust and understanding within your relationships. When you communicate your needs directly, you significantly reduce the likelihood of misunderstandings, resentment, or feelings of being taken advantage of. This clarity allows you and your loved ones to navigate challenges and conflicts more constructively, as you have a shared understanding of each other's boundaries and priorities.

For instance, if you feel overwhelmed by certain responsibilities, openly expressing this to your partner can lead to a collaborative approach in sharing tasks. Such transparency not only alleviates your burdens but also strengthens the bond you share, as both parties work together to create a more balanced dynamic.

Strengthening Emotional & Psychological Safety

Furthermore, self advocacy strengthens the emotional and psychological safety within your relationships. By setting clear boundaries and standing firm in your needs, you demonstrate that you respect yourself and expect the same from others. This mutual respect creates an environment where individuals feel safe to express their feelings and advocate for their own needs.

In this supportive atmosphere, your loved ones are encouraged to also advocate for themselves. This reciprocal dynamic fosters a culture of mutual care, respect, and support, where everyone feels valued and empowered. As each person learns to voice their needs, the relationship grows stronger and becomes more resilient.

Navigating Resistance & Encouraging Growth

As you engage in self advocacy, you may encounter resistance or pushback from others who are accustomed to you prioritizing their needs over your own. This resistance often stems from established patterns in relationships where one person's needs have historically taken precedence. However, by remaining steadfast in your self advocacy, you have the opportunity to transform these relationships in profound ways.

Your willingness to have difficult conversations and maintain your boundaries can inspire growth, empathy, and a deeper appreciation for each person's individuality. When you model self advocacy, you encourage others to evaluate their own willingness to express their needs. This can lead to a transformative shift in the relationship, allowing both parties to engage in a more balanced and supportive manner.

Fostering Mutual Empowerment

Ultimately, self advocacy is a gift you give not only to yourself but also to the people in your life. By empowering yourself to voice your needs and preferences, you create the conditions for more authentic, fulfilling, and mutually supportive relationships to thrive.

As you embrace self advocacy, consider the following practices to enhance your relationships further:

Communicate Regularly

Make it a habit to check in with your loved ones about their needs and feelings while sharing your own. Regular communication fosters a culture of openness.

Practice Active Listening

When advocating for yourself, also practice active listening. This shows that you value the perspectives of others, creating a balanced dialogue.

Encourage Vulnerability

Create a safe space where your loved ones feel comfortable expressing their needs. Encourage them to share their thoughts and feelings without fear of judgment.

Celebrate Each Other's Voices

Acknowledge and celebrate instances when your loved ones advocate for themselves. This reinforces the importance of self advocacy and fosters a supportive environment.

Adapt & Grow Together

Be open to feedback and willing to adapt as your relationships evolve. Growth is a shared journey, and navigating changes together can strengthen your bond.

By integrating these practices into your relationships, you can cultivate a deeper sense of connection and understanding. Self advocacy not only enhances your own well-being but also enriches the lives of those around you, leading to healthier, more fulfilling relationships built on a foundation of respect and mutual support.

Increased Opportunities: The Impact Of Self Advocacy In Professional Settings

In professional settings, self advocacy can be a powerful tool for unlocking new opportunities and advancing your career. When you confidently express your ideas, skills, and accomplishments, you position yourself as a valuable contributor who deserves recognition and advancement.

This proactive approach can significantly alter the trajectory of your career, leading to greater satisfaction and success.

Positioning Yourself for Success

By advocating for yourself, you challenge the tendency to remain passive or wait to be "discovered." Many professionals fall into the trap of believing that hard work alone will lead to recognition and advancement. However, self advocacy empowers you to take an active role in shining a light on your strengths and capabilities, ensuring that your unique talents and potential are not overlooked.

For example, if you successfully lead a project or achieve significant results, it's essential to communicate these accomplishments to your team and superiors. By doing so, you not only highlight your contributions but also reinforce your commitment to the organization's goals. This visibility can open doors to new projects, promotions, or even career-changing opportunities that may have otherwise eluded you.

Demonstrating Engagement & Ambition

Self advocacy also demonstrates to your colleagues and superiors that you are engaged, ambitious, and committed to your professional growth. When you advocate for yourself, you show that you are willing to take the initiative, speak up, and champion your own interests. This self assurance can be a powerful differentiator, setting you apart from those who may be more hesitant to advocate for themselves.

In team meetings, for instance, sharing your insights or suggesting innovative ideas not only showcases your expertise but also positions you as a thought leader within your organization. Colleagues and managers are more likely to recognize and consider you for new opportunities when they see you actively participating and contributing to discussions.

Navigating Workplace Dynamics

Furthermore, self advocacy can help you navigate challenging workplace dynamics and power imbalances more effectively. When you are able to clearly articulate your needs, concerns, and ideas, you are better equipped to navigate conflicts, negotiate for fair compensation, and ensure that your contributions are appropriately recognized and rewarded.

For example, if you feel that your workload is unmanageable or that your contributions are not being acknowledged, self advocacy enables you to approach your supervisor with constructive feedback. By expressing your concerns calmly and confidently, you create space for dialogue and potential solutions, fostering a healthier work environment.

The Art of Constructive Communication

It's important to note that self advocacy in the workplace does not mean being aggressive or confrontational. Instead, it involves communicating your thoughts and needs in a calm, confident, and constructive manner.

Here are some strategies to effectively advocate for yourself while maintaining positive relationships:

Prepare Your Talking Points

Before discussions or meetings, outline key points you want to address. This preparation helps you articulate your thoughts clearly and confidently.

Choose the Right Time & Place

Timing is crucial when advocating for yourself. Approach conversations when your manager or colleagues are receptive, ensuring that you have their full attention.

Use "I" Statements

Frame your needs and concerns using "I" statements to express how situations affect you personally. For instance, "I feel overwhelmed with my current workload and would appreciate discussing how we can redistribute tasks."

Listen Actively

Advocacy is a two-way street. Be open to feedback and listen to the perspectives of others. This approach fosters mutual respect and understanding.

Follow Up

After advocating for yourself, follow up on any agreements or discussions. This demonstrates your commitment and keeps the lines of communication open.

The Ripple Effect of Self Advocacy

As you cultivate the habit of self advocacy in your professional life, you may find that the skills and confidence you develop have a positive ripple effect on other areas of your life as well. The ability to stand up for yourself and articulate your value can translate to increased opportunities, both within and outside of your career.

Self advocacy encourages you to seek out new challenges, embark on personal growth endeavors, and explore passions that may have previously been sidelined. Whether it's pursuing further education, engaging in community initiatives, or exploring entrepreneurial ventures, the confidence gained from advocating for yourself can inspire you to take bold steps in various aspects of your life.

Conclusion: Embrace Your Power

Self advocacy is a vital skill that can dramatically enhance your professional journey. By confidently expressing your ideas and asserting your needs, you unlock a world of opportunities that align with your talents and aspirations. This practice not only fosters personal growth but also contributes to a more dynamic, engaged, and empowered workplace culture.

Embrace self advocacy as a powerful tool in your career toolkit. As you practice this skill, remember that you are not just advocating for yourself; you are also paving the way for others to do the same, fostering an environment of mutual respect and support. With each step you take in advocating for yourself, you are investing in a future filled with greater opportunities, fulfillment, and success.

Conflict Resolution: Harnessing Self Advocacy For Effective Communication

Self advocacy equips you with the essential tools to navigate conflicts and disagreements more effectively. When you are able to clearly articulate your feelings, needs, and boundaries, you are better prepared to address challenges in a constructive manner. This proactive approach not only fosters healthier resolutions but also prevents misunderstandings that can escalate tensions and damage relationships.

The Role of Assertive Communication

At the core of self advocacy in conflict resolution is the ability to communicate assertively. Assertive communication involves expressing your thoughts and feelings openly and honestly while respecting the perspectives of others.

Here are some key components of assertive communication that can enhance your conflict resolution skills:

Use "I" Statements

Instead of blaming or accusing, frame your concerns using "I" statements. For example, say "I feel overwhelmed when deadlines are unclear" rather than "You never give me clear deadlines." This approach helps convey your feelings without putting the other person on the defensive.

Maintain A Calm & Confident Tone

Your tone of voice can significantly impact how your message is received. Speak calmly and confidently, which helps convey that you are serious about your needs while remaining approachable.

Active Listening

Demonstrate that you value the other person's perspective by actively listening. This involves not only hearing their words but also understanding their feelings and concerns. Reflect back what you've heard to confirm understanding, such as, "It sounds like you are feeling frustrated about the project timeline."

Creating a Respectful Environment

By employing these communication techniques, you create an environment of mutual respect and understanding. This atmosphere helps diffuse tension and encourages collaborative problem-solving rather than escalating the conflict. When both parties feel heard and respected, they are more likely to engage in constructive dialogue and work towards a solution that satisfies everyone involved.

Standing Firm in Your Needs

Self advocacy empowers you to stand firm in your needs and boundaries, even in the face of opposition or resistance. When you are clear about what is and is not acceptable to you, you can navigate conflicts without compromising your values or well-being. This self assurance is crucial in preventing you from being steamrolled or coerced into agreements that do not serve your best interests.

For instance, if a colleague continually interrupts you during meetings, self advocacy allows you to address this behavior directly. You might say, "I appreciate your enthusiasm, but I would like to finish my point before we discuss further." By asserting your need for respect, you reinforce your boundaries and foster a more equitable dialogue.

Transforming Dynamics Through Self Advocacy

Self advocacy during conflicts reinforces the belief that your voice and experiences matter. By refusing to be silenced or dismissed, you send a powerful message that your needs deserve to be heard and addressed. This commitment to self advocacy can have a transformative effect on the dynamics of your relationships, shifting them from one of imbalance or disrespect to one of mutual consideration and problem-solving. When you actively participate in resolving conflicts, you model healthy communication patterns for others. This not only sets a standard for how you expect to be treated but also encourages those around you to engage in similar self advocacy, fostering a culture of respect and collaboration.

Collaboration Over Competition

It's important to note that self advocacy in conflict resolution is not about winning at all costs or stubbornly refusing to compromise. Instead, it is about finding a balance between standing up for your needs and being open to mutually beneficial solutions. This collaborative approach allows you to engage in conflicts with a spirit of cooperation and a willingness to reach a resolution that honors the concerns of all parties involved.

Consider a scenario where two team members disagree on the direction of a project. Rather than insisting on your viewpoint, you might say, "I understand your perspective, and I think we can find a way to incorporate both our ideas. Let's brainstorm together." This willingness to collaborate not only resolves the immediate conflict but also strengthens the relationship between team members.

The Ripple Effect on Relationships

As you practice self advocacy in conflict resolution, you may find that the skills and confidence you develop have a positive impact on the quality of your relationships. By navigating disagreements with assertiveness and empathy, you can strengthen trust, respect, and communication within your connections. This leads to more fulfilling and harmonious interactions, where all parties feel valued and understood.

The Empowerment Journey

By deeply understanding the transformative power of self advocacy in these key areas of your life, you can cultivate the courage and conviction to become your own champion. Embracing self advocacy empowers you to take control of your life, enhance your self worth, build healthier relationships, access new opportunities, and navigate conflicts more effectively.

This journey of self empowerment is a profound expression of self love and a pathway to a more authentic, fulfilling, and purposeful life. As you continue to practice these skills, you will not only improve your ability to resolve conflicts but also enhance your overall quality of life, leading to greater satisfaction in both personal and professional realms. Embrace the power of self advocacy as a vital tool for navigating conflicts, and watch as it transforms both your relationships and your sense of self.

Techniques For Assertive Communication: Mastering the Art Of Self Advocacy

Assertive communication is a key component of self advocacy, enabling you to express your thoughts, feelings, and needs in a clear and respectful manner. By mastering these techniques, you can become more confident and effective in advocating for yourself, ultimately leading to healthier relationships and improved outcomes in various areas of your life.

Use "I" Statements

Framing your communication using "I" statements is a powerful tool for assertive self expression. Instead of making accusatory or blaming statements, such as "You never listen to me," try saying, "I feel unheard when I try to share my ideas." This approach shifts the focus away from the other person's actions and onto your own feelings and needs, reducing the likelihood of defensiveness.

Benefits of "I" Statements

Ownership of Emotions

"I" statements allow you to take ownership of your emotions, rather than projecting them onto the other person. This fosters a more constructive dialogue.

Encouraging Empathy

By expressing your feelings and needs without blame, you create an opportunity for the other person to understand your perspective and respond with empathy.

Reducing Confrontation

This method makes the conversation less confrontational, as it emphasizes your personal experience rather than criticizing the other person's behavior.

Consistently using "I" statements can enhance your ability to communicate your needs and concerns effectively, setting the stage for more constructive dialogue and problem-solving.

Be Clear & Specific

When advocating for yourself, clarity and specificity in your communication are paramount. Vague or ambiguous statements can lead to misunderstandings and hinder effective responses.

Example of Clarity

Instead of saying, "I need more support," you might say, "I would appreciate it if we could set aside time each week to discuss our projects together." This specificity ensures that your message is understood and highlights your needs clearly.

Importance of Clarity

Clarity and specificity can be particularly important in professional settings, where ambiguity or vagueness may be interpreted as a lack of preparedness or commitment. By communicating with precision, you position yourself as a confident and competent advocate for your needs and interests.

Demonstrates Preparedness

Being clear and specific shows that you have thoughtfully considered your request and understand what you need.

Enhances Understanding

Clear communication reduces the risk of misinterpretation, making it easier for others to respond appropriately.

Professionalism

In professional settings, precise communication is often interpreted as a sign of competence and commitment, positioning you as a confident advocate for your interests.

Maintain A Calm & Confident Tone

The tone of your voice significantly impacts how your message is received. Speaking in a calm and confident manner helps convey self assurance and can diffuse potential tension in conversations.

Practicing Calmness

Practicing a steady, measured tone can take some effort, especially in high-stakes or emotionally charged situations. However, this skill is essential for effective self advocacy. By remaining poised and composed, you demonstrate your commitment to finding a constructive resolution, rather than escalating the conflict.

Stay Composed

Maintain a steady, measured tone, especially in emotionally charged situations. This demonstrates your commitment to finding constructive resolutions rather than escalating conflicts.

Focus On Clarity

A calm tone allows you to articulate your thoughts more clearly, helping you maintain emotional control and clarity of thought.

By consistently practicing a calm and confident tone, you can enhance the effectiveness of your self advocacy efforts and contribute to more positive interactions.

Practice Active Listening

Assertive communication is a two-way street, and active listening is a crucial component of this dynamic. When advocating for yourself, it's important to express your needs clearly while demonstrating that you value the other person's perspective.

Active Listening Techniques

Engage Fully

Make eye contact, nod in acknowledgment, and use verbal affirmations to show that you are engaged in the conversation.

Paraphrase & Summarize

Reflect back what the other person has said to confirm your understanding. For example, "So, what I hear you saying is that you feel overwhelmed with the current workload."

Benefits of Active Listening

Fosters Mutual Respect

By genuinely considering the other person's perspective, you create an atmosphere of respect and open communication.

Enhances Your Advocacy

Understanding the other person's concerns allows you to tailor your self advocacy approach, leading to more constructive negotiations.

Builds Trust

Demonstrating that you value the other person's input can strengthen trust and collaboration in your relationships.

Set Boundaries Clearly

Setting clear boundaries is essential when advocating for yourself. Communicating your limits in a direct yet respectful manner reinforces your needs and ensures that your limits are respected.

Example of Boundary Setting

If someone frequently interrupts you during meetings, you could say, "I appreciate your input, but I would like to finish my thought before we discuss it further." This establishes a boundary around your contributions.

Importance of Boundary Setting

It's important to remember that setting boundaries is not about being confrontational or aggressive. Rather, it is about honoring your own needs and preferences in a way that allows for productive and harmonious interactions. When you communicate your boundaries calmly and firmly, you demonstrate self respect and self care, which can inspire others to do the same.

Promotes Mutual Understanding

Clear boundaries help create an understanding of each other's limits, preventing future misunderstandings and resentment.

Demonstrates Self Respect

Communicating your boundaries calmly and firmly shows that you honor your own needs and preferences, which can inspire others to do the same.

Enhances Self Confidence

Consistently maintaining your boundaries reinforces their importance and builds your self confidence, further empowering your self advocacy efforts.

Be Open to Feedback

Remaining open to feedback from others is essential when advocating for yourself. This openness demonstrates a willingness to engage in constructive dialogue and fosters mutual respect.

How To Be Open to Feedback

Listen Actively

Pay attention to the perspectives and concerns of others without interrupting. This shows that you value their input.

Consider Input Thoughtfully

While you don't have to agree with all feedback, be willing to reflect on it and determine if any adjustments to your approach could be beneficial.

Benefits of Openness

It's important to strike a balance between standing firm in your boundaries and being open to constructive input. You don't have to agree with everything that is suggested, but you should be willing to listen, reflect, and determine if any adjustments to your approach could be beneficial.

Encourages Collaboration

Being receptive to feedback can lead to a more collaborative approach to problem-solving, where everyone feels their voice is valued.

Refines Your Approach

Feedback can reveal blind spots or alternative solutions, making your self advocacy efforts more nuanced and effective.

Builds Trust

Demonstrating a willingness to consider others' input fosters deeper connections and trust in your relationships.

Practice Assertiveness in Low-Stakes Situations

If you find assertive communication challenging, start practicing in low-stakes situations before tackling higher-stakes scenarios. This gradual approach can help build your confidence and skills.

Examples of Low-Stakes Situations

Casual Conversations

Express your preferences in everyday discussions, such as choosing a restaurant or planning a weekend activity.

Everyday Requests

Practice asking for small favors, like requesting help with a task or suggesting a change in plans.

Benefits of Low-Stakes Practice

Practicing assertiveness in low-stakes situations also provides an opportunity to receive immediate feedback and adjust your approach as needed. If you encounter resistance or feel that your message was not received as intended, you can reflect on what worked, what could be improved, and how you might handle the situation differently next time.

Builds Confidence

These smaller interactions allow you to experiment with assertive communication techniques without the pressure of high-stakes outcomes.

Immediate Feedback

You can receive immediate feedback and adjust your approach as needed, helping you refine your assertiveness skills.

Gradual Expansion

As you become more comfortable asserting yourself in low-stakes situations, you'll be better prepared to apply these techniques in more significant contexts.

Visualize Successful Outcomes

Another powerful technique for enhancing your assertiveness is to visualize successful outcomes before entering a conversation where you need to advocate for yourself.

Visualization Techniques

Close Your Eyes

Take a moment to visualize yourself communicating your needs confidently and respectfully.

Imagine Positive Reactions

Picture the other person listening attentively and responding with openness and understanding.

Rehearse Responses

Mentally rehearse how you will handle potential challenges or pushback, reinforcing your preparedness.

Benefits of Visualization

Visualization also allows you to anticipate potential challenges or obstacles you may face, and to practice how you will navigate them. By mentally rehearsing how you will respond to pushback or resistance, you can feel better prepared to handle those situations in real life.

Reduces Anxiety

Visualizing a positive outcome can help reduce anxiety and boost your self confidence, making it easier to access your assertive communication skills.

Prepares For Challenges

Anticipating obstacles allows you to feel more equipped to navigate them when they arise in real life.

Reinforces Belief in Your Abilities

This mental rehearsal reinforces the belief that you have the skills and capabilities to advocate for yourself effectively

By combining these techniques—using "I" statements, being clear and specific, maintaining a calm tone, practicing active listening, setting boundaries, being open to feedback, practicing in low-stakes situations, and visualizing success—you can enhance your assertive communication skills. This mastery will empower you to advocate for yourself more confidently and effectively, leading to healthier relationships and positive outcomes in all areas of your life. Remember, assertiveness is a skill that takes time and practice to develop, so be patient with yourself and celebrate your progress along the way.

Becoming Your Own Champion: Conclusion

Becoming your own champion through self advocacy is a powerful manifestation of self love and empowerment. By standing up for your needs and communicating assertively, you actively create a life that mirrors your values and desires. Remember, advocating for yourself is not a selfish act; it is an essential expression of honoring your worth and nurturing healthy relationships.

As you practice self advocacy and assertive communication, be patient with yourself. This journey may require time and effort, but each step you take toward becoming your own champion reinforces your self love and confidence. Embrace your voice, affirm your needs, and celebrate the empowerment that comes with advocating for yourself. By doing so, you lay the groundwork for a life that is not only more fulfilling but also more authentic.

The path of self advocacy may present challenges, but the rewards are profound. Cultivating the courage to stand up for yourself unlocks a deeper sense of personal agency, self worth, and the ability to shape the life you truly desire. Each time you assert your needs, set a boundary, or communicate your perspective with clarity and conviction, you reinforce the belief that you are deserving of respect, consideration, and the fulfillment of your aspirations.

Embrace this transformative journey of becoming your own champion. Allow it to serve as a testament to the self love that resides within you, guiding you toward a life rich with authenticity, purpose, and meaningful connections.

As you continue to advocate for yourself, remember that you are not alone; you are part of a powerful movement of individuals reclaiming their voices and creating a world that honors the inherent dignity and worth of all people.

So, take that first step—whether it's expressing a preference in a casual conversation or addressing a long-standing issue in a relationship. Each act of self advocacy, no matter how small, is a victory worth celebrating. For in doing so, you not only empower yourself but also inspire those around you to do the same, rippling outward and contributing to a more just, equitable, and compassionate world.

As you progress on this journey, remain committed to practicing the techniques of assertive communication. By mastering these skills, you enhance not only your self advocacy efforts but also the quality of your relationships and the opportunities available to you. Embrace your power, champion your needs, and watch as your life transforms into a reflection of your true self.

Chapter 7: Living Authentically

Embracing Your True Self

To live authentically, we must first embrace our true selves. This involves acknowledging our unique qualities, values, and passions without reservation. Here are some steps to guide you on this journey:

Self Reflection

Take time to reflect on what truly matters to you. What are your core values? What ignites your passions? Consider journaling your thoughts or engaging in creative activities that allow you to express your inner self. This self awareness will serve as a compass, guiding you toward choices that resonate with your authentic being.

Let Go of Expectations

Society often imposes expectations that can lead us away from our true selves. Challenge the notion of "fitting in" and release the fear of judgment. Understand that your worth is not contingent upon meeting external standards. Embrace the freedom that comes with letting go of these constraints.

Celebrate Your Uniqueness

Rather than comparing yourself to others, celebrate what makes you unique. Acknowledge your quirks, strengths, and even perceived flaws. These aspects contribute to the beautiful tapestry of who you are. Surround yourself with people who appreciate and uplift your individuality.

Cultivating Authentic Connections

Living authentically extends beyond ourselves; it also influences the relationships we cultivate. Here's how to nurture authentic connections with others:

Open Communication

Foster an environment of honesty and openness in your relationships. Share your thoughts, feelings, and needs with those you trust. This vulnerability encourages others to do the same, creating deeper and more meaningful connections.

Set Boundaries

Establishing healthy boundaries is crucial for maintaining authenticity. Communicate your limits clearly and assertively. This not only protects your well-being but also allows others to understand and respect your true self.

Surround Yourself With Support

Seek out relationships that inspire and empower you. Surround yourself with individuals who encourage your authenticity and celebrate your successes. These positive influences will nourish your journey toward living authentically.

Continuous Growth In Authenticity

As we explore these strategies, remember that living authentically is an ongoing process. It requires patience, self compassion, and a willingness to embrace change. Here are a few additional practices to help you nurture your authentic self:

Mindfulness Practice

Engage in mindfulness exercises to remain present and attuned to your thoughts and feelings. This awareness can help you make choices that align with your true self.

Seek Feedback

Don't hesitate to ask trusted friends or mentors for feedback on your journey toward authenticity. Their perspectives can provide valuable insights and encouragement.

Celebrate Progress

Acknowledge and celebrate your progress along the way, no matter how small. Each step toward authenticity is a victory worth recognizing.

Overcoming Obstacles To Authenticity

While the journey toward embracing authenticity is rewarding, it may also present challenges. Here are some common obstacles and how to overcome them:

Fear of Rejection

The fear of being rejected for who we truly are can be paralyzing. To combat this, remind yourself that those who truly matter will appreciate you for your authenticity. Embrace the idea that being true to yourself may attract the right people into your life.

Self Doubt

Self doubt can hinder our ability to express our authentic selves. Combat this by practicing self compassion and affirming your worth. Surround yourself with supportive individuals who uplift your confidence.

Comparison

In a world dominated by social media, it's easy to fall into the trap of comparison. Remember that everyone's journey is unique. Focus on your own path and celebrate your individual milestones, free from the weight of comparison.

Conclusion: A Life Of Authenticity

Embracing authenticity is not only a gift to ourselves but also to those around us. By living true to who we are, we invite others to do the same, fostering a world filled with genuine connections and mutual respect. As you continue on this path, remember that self love and authenticity are intertwined, each nurturing and reinforcing the other.

By committing to this journey, you are choosing to honor your true self and live a life that reflects your core values and passions. May this chapter inspire you to embrace your true self fully and live a life rich with authenticity and love. As you embark on this transformative journey, let the light of your authenticity shine brightly, illuminating the path for yourself and others along the way.

Chapter 8: Self Acceptance & Self Compassion In Relationships

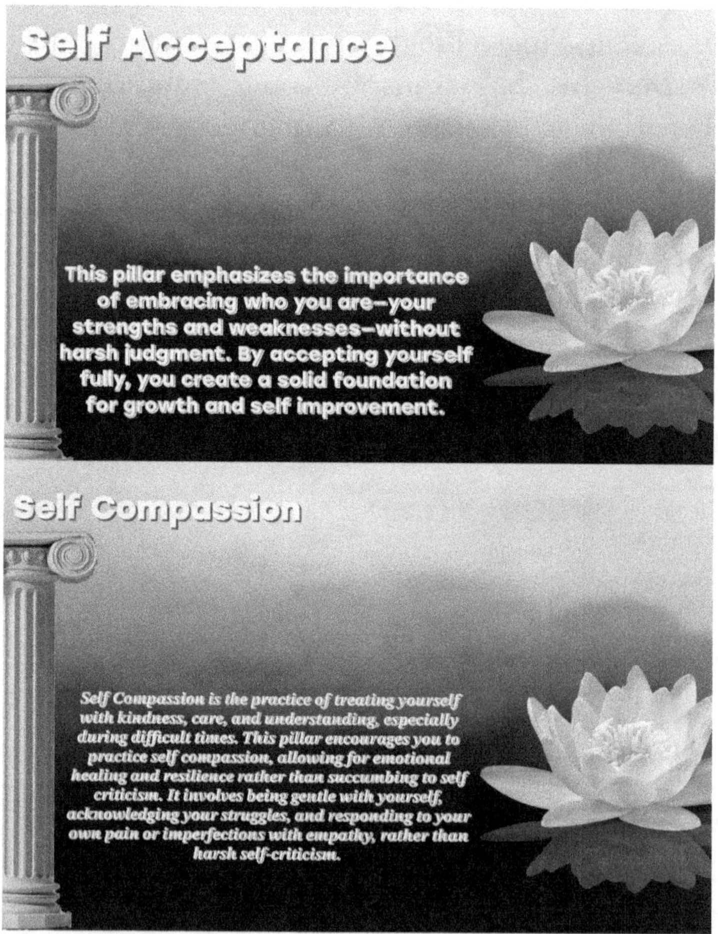

Introduction

As we continue our journey of self love, it becomes clear that the principles of self acceptance and self compassion hold profound significance not only for our own personal growth, but also for the quality of our relationships. When we learn to embrace ourselves with kindness and understanding, we create the foundation for more authentic, fulfilling, and mutually supportive connections with the people in our lives.

Power Of Self Acceptance In Relationships

Self acceptance is the foundation upon which healthy relationships are built. When we can fully accept ourselves, flaws and all, we send a powerful message to those around us: "I am worthy of love and respect, exactly as I am." This self assurance creates an environment where others feel safe to be their authentic selves as well.

Conversely, when we struggle with self acceptance, we may unconsciously project an image of ourselves that is inauthentic or constantly seeking validation from our partners, friends, and loved ones. This can lead to an imbalance of power within the relationship, where we place an unhealthy dependence on others to fill the void of self love.

By cultivating self acceptance, we free ourselves and our loved ones from this dynamic. We no longer need others to affirm our worth or complete us; instead, we can show up in our relationships as whole, secure individuals who have the capacity to give and receive love in a healthy, balanced way.

Self acceptance also allows us to be more transparent and vulnerable with our partners. When we are not constantly trying to hide or fix our perceived flaws, we can engage in more meaningful, intimate conversations. This openness fosters deeper connections, as both parties feel safe to share their authentic selves without fear of judgment or rejection.

Self acceptance enables us to set healthy boundaries in our relationships. We are less likely to tolerate disrespect, manipulation, or behavior that undermines our self worth. Instead, we can clearly communicate our needs and expectations, confident in the knowledge that we deserve to be treated with care and consideration.

Strategies for Cultivating Self Acceptance in Relationships

Here are some of the best strategies for cultivating self acceptance within the context of relationships:

Practice Self Compassion

Extend the same kindness and understanding to yourself that you would offer a dear friend. When you make a mistake or feel insecure, respond with self empathy rather than harsh self criticism. This self compassion can help counteract the tendency to be overly self critical in your relationships.

Celebrate Your Unique Qualities

Identify and appreciate the special traits, talents, and experiences that make you who you are. Recognize how these unique aspects of yourself contribute positively to your relationships, rather than viewing them as flaws to be hidden or changed.

Reframe Imperfections

Acknowledge that no person or relationship is perfect. Shift your perspective to view your (and your partner's) imperfections as opportunities for growth, rather than as reasons to feel inadequate. Embrace the messy, human elements of your connections.

Practice Gratitude

Express gratitude for your partner, friends, and loved ones, focusing on what you appreciate about them rather than comparing yourself. This shifts the mindset from lack to abundance, helping you feel more secure in your own self worth.

Set Healthy Boundaries

Communicate your needs and limits clearly, without apology. Honoring your boundaries demonstrates self acceptance and shows your loved ones how you expect to be treated. This empowers you to engage in relationships on equal footing.

Share Your Vulnerabilities

Open up about your insecurities, mistakes, and areas of growth with trusted loved ones. Allowing yourself to be seen in your imperfect humanity can deepen intimacy and mutual understanding in your relationships.

Surround Yourself With Supportive People

Cultivate relationships with individuals who accept and appreciate you as you are. Limit time with those who are critical or undermine your self acceptance. The company you keep can significantly impact your ability to feel worthy in your connections.

Engage in Self Care

Make time for activities that nurture your mind, body, and spirit. When you prioritize your own well-being, you demonstrate that you are worthy of care and attention - a powerful message to convey in your relationships.

By implementing these strategies, you create an upward spiral where self acceptance begets more self acceptance, both within yourself and in your relationships. This foundation of self love allows you to engage with your loved ones from a place of wholeness, authenticity, and mutual respect.

Role Of Self Compassion In Relationships

Alongside self acceptance, self compassion plays a vital role in nurturing fulfilling relationships. Self compassion involves treating ourselves with the same kindness, understanding, and empathy that we would extend to a dear friend. When we cultivate this quality within ourselves, it naturally overflows into our interactions with others.

By practicing self compassion, we learn to approach our own mistakes, failures, and shortcomings with a gentle, non-judgmental mindset. This self kindness allows us to bounce back from setbacks more quickly, rather than getting mired in self criticism or shame. As we extend this same grace to ourselves, we become better equipped to offer it to our loved ones as well.

Self compassion also helps us to avoid the trap of comparison, which can be so damaging to relationships. When we are able to celebrate our own unique journey and appreciate the diverse paths of those around us, we create an environment of mutual support and encouragement, rather than competition or envy.

Self compassion fosters empathy and understanding within our relationships. As we learn to view our own struggles with compassion, we naturally develop the capacity to empathize with the challenges faced by our partners, friends, and family members. This empathy enables us to respond with patience, kindness, and a genuine desire to support one another through life's ups and downs.

Strategies for Cultivating Self Compassion in Relationships

Integrating self compassion into our relationships requires a consistent, intentional practice. Here are some strategies that can help:

Practice Self Empathy

When a conflict or challenge arises in a relationship, take a step back and tune into your own emotional experience. Ask yourself, "How would I treat a dear friend who was going through this?" Then, extend that same empathy and understanding to yourself.

Avoid Comparisons

Resist the urge to compare your relationship or your partner to others. Celebrate the unique qualities and dynamics that make your connection special, rather than trying to measure up to external standards.

Let Go of Perfectionism

Recognize that no relationship is perfect, and that striving for flawlessness will only lead to disappointment and disillusionment. Embrace the messiness and imperfections as opportunities for growth and deeper understanding.

Communicate Openly

Share your struggles and vulnerabilities with your partner or loved ones. Allow them to witness your humanity and respond with compassion, rather than keeping up appearances.

Offer Forgiveness

When mistakes or hurts occur within the relationship, cultivate the capacity to forgive. This doesn't mean condoning harmful behavior, but rather releasing the need for retribution and creating space for healing.

Celebrate Progress

Acknowledge and appreciate the small steps of growth and healing that occur within your relationships. Celebrate the moments when you or your loved ones demonstrate self compassion, as these are the building blocks of a more fulfilling connection.

By weaving self acceptance and self compassion into the fabric of our relationships, we create an environment that is conducive to authentic connection, mutual understanding, and enduring love. As we extend the same kindness to ourselves that we wish to receive from others, we open the door to relationships that are truly nourishing and transformative.

The journey of self love is not meant to be undertaken in isolation; rather, it is a path that can and should be shared with the important people in our lives. When we model self acceptance and self compassion, we inspire those around us to do the same, ultimately contributing to a world where we all feel safe to be our truest selves.

Importance Of Cultivating Self Acceptance & Self Compassion In Relationships

Cultivating self acceptance and self compassion is essential for fostering healthy, fulfilling relationships for several key reasons:

Authenticity & Vulnerability

When we accept and have compassion for ourselves, we are more able to show up authentically in our relationships. We no longer feel the need to hide or suppress our true selves, and can instead engage with our loved ones from a place of vulnerability and transparency. This openness lays the foundation for deeper, more meaningful connections.

Balanced Power Dynamics

Individuals who struggle with self acceptance often seek validation and completion from their partners, creating an unhealthy power imbalance. By developing self love, we become whole within ourselves and can enter relationships as equal partners, rather than relying on others to fill our internal voids. This balance allows for mutual respect and support to flourish.

Healthy Boundaries

Self acceptance empowers us to set clear boundaries and communicate our needs effectively. We are less likely to tolerate disrespect or behavior that undermines our self worth, and can advocate for ourselves with confidence. Healthy boundaries create an environment of mutual understanding and trust within our relationships.

Empathy & Compassion

As we cultivate self compassion, we become more attuned to the struggles and experiences of others. This empathy allows us to respond to our loved ones with kindness, patience, and a genuine desire to support them through life's challenges. Extending the same compassion we give ourselves to our partners and friends strengthens the emotional intimacy and resilience of the relationship.

Resilience in Conflict

When we approach our own mistakes and shortcomings with self compassion, we become better equipped to navigate conflicts and challenges within our relationships. Rather than getting mired in shame or defensiveness, we can work through issues with a spirit of understanding and a commitment to finding mutually beneficial solutions.

Modeling Self Love

By embodying self acceptance and self compassion, we set a powerful example for our loved ones. We inspire them to treat themselves and others with greater kindness, and contribute to a culture of mutual support and respect within our relationships and communities.

Reduced Relational Conflicts

When we have self acceptance and self compassion, we are less likely to project our own insecurities and self criticisms onto our partners or loved ones. This reduces the potential for conflicts that arise from a lack of self love, such as excessive neediness, jealousy, or controlling behaviors.

Greater Capacity for Forgiveness

Self compassion allows us to be more forgiving - both of ourselves and of others. When we can extend grace to ourselves for our own mistakes and imperfections, we are more likely to do the same for our loved ones. This fosters an environment where ruptures can be repaired and relationships can deepen through the process of forgiveness.

Enhanced Emotional Intimacy

Self acceptance and self compassion enable us to be more emotionally vulnerable and intimate with our partners. When we can fully show up as we are, without the need for masks or pretenses, we create the safety for our loved ones to do the same. This reciprocal vulnerability is the foundation for profound emotional connection.

Improved Communication

Individuals with self acceptance and self compassion tend to communicate more effectively in their relationships. They are better able to express their needs, boundaries, and feelings in a clear and non-defensive manner. This open communication promotes mutual understanding and reduces the risk of misunderstandings.

Positive Role Modeling for Children

When parents or caregivers demonstrate self acceptance and self compassion, they provide a powerful example for the children in their lives. This modeling teaches young people that they are worthy of love and kindness, and empowers them to treat themselves and others with greater compassion as they grow.

Strengthened Support Systems

Individuals who have cultivated self love are often better able to build and maintain supportive social networks. They are more likely to attract and retain friendships and relationships with people who share their values of mutual respect and acceptance. This strong support system can be a crucial resource during challenging times.

Ultimately, the cultivation of self acceptance and self compassion is not just an individual pursuit, but one that has a profound impact on the quality and depth of our relationships. When we learn to love and care for ourselves, we create the fertile ground for truly nourishing, authentic connections to take root and thrive.

Reflective Questions

1. How do I currently view and accept myself within my
relationships? _______________________________________

____

____

____

Do I feel worthy of love and respect from my partner, friends,
and family? _______________________________________

____

____

____

____

2. In what ways have my struggles with self acceptance
impacted my relationships? _______________________________

____

____

____

____

Have I found myself seeking validation or constantly trying to
prove my worth to others? _______________________________

____

____

____

____

____

____

3. When I make mistakes or face challenges in my
relationships, how do I typically respond to myself?

____

____

Do I tend to be self critical, or can I extend the same
compassion to myself that I would to a loved one? __________

____

____

4. How open and vulnerable am I able to be with my partner
or close friends?

____

____

Does the fear of being "found out" prevent me from fully
sharing my authentic self? _______________________________

____

____

5. Do I have clear boundaries in my relationships, or do I often
sacrifice my own needs to please others? _________________

____

____

How could cultivating self acceptance help me communicate
my boundaries more effectively? _________________________

____

____

____

6. When I witness my partner or loved ones struggling, am I able to respond with empathy and understanding? _________

____

____

How might developing self compassion enhance my capacity for compassion towards others? ___________________________

____

____

7. In what ways do I currently compare myself or my relationships to external standards or the experiences of others? ____

____

 How could letting go of this tendency foster more appreciation for the unique dynamics in my own connections?

____

____

8. What self care practices or rituals help me nurture self acceptance and self compassion? ___________________________

____

____

How can I intentionally weave these into my relationships to create an environment of mutual care and support?

____

____

____

9. Who in my life currently models self acceptance and self compassion in a way that inspires me?

____

____

____

How can I learn from their example to strengthen these qualities within myself?

____

____

____

10. As I continue this journey of self love, what specific goals do I have for enhancing the self acceptance and self compassion within my relationships?

____

____

____

What tangible steps can I take to work towards these goals?

____

____

____

____

Engaging with these reflective questions can help you gain deeper insight into the role of self acceptance and self compassion in your relationships, and inspire you to take meaningful action towards cultivating these transformative qualities.

Chapter Conclusion: Self Acceptance & Self Compassion In Relationships

As we reach the end of this chapter on self acceptance and self compassion in relationships, it's clear that these two essential elements of self love hold the power to transform not only our personal lives, but also the quality and depth of our connections with others.

When we cultivate self acceptance - the ability to fully embrace ourselves, flaws and all - we send a powerful message to those around us. We communicate that we are worthy of love and respect, exactly as we are. This self assurance creates an environment where our partners, friends, and loved ones feel safe to show up authentically as well. It lays the foundation for relationships built on mutual understanding, transparency, and balanced power dynamics.

Alongside self acceptance, self compassion plays a vital role in nurturing fulfilling connections. By treating ourselves with the same kindness, empathy, and understanding that we would extend to a dear friend, we develop the capacity to respond to our own mistakes and shortcomings with grace. This self kindness, in turn, overflows into our interactions with others, fostering greater emotional intimacy, resilience in the face of conflict, and a genuine desire to support one another through life's challenges.

As we have explored the strategies for cultivating self acceptance and self compassion within our relationships, a clear picture has emerged. These qualities empower us to communicate our needs and boundaries effectively, celebrate the unique gifts we each bring to our connections, and approach the inevitable imperfections of relationships with a spirit of growth and understanding.

Ultimately, the journey of self love is not meant to be undertaken in isolation. When we model self acceptance and self compassion, we inspire those around us to do the same, contributing to a world where we all feel safe to be our truest selves. By weaving these transformative principles into the fabric of our relationships, we create the fertile ground for nourishing, authentic connections to take root and thrive.

So, as you continue forward on this path of self discovery and relational growth, remember that self acceptance and self compassion are not merely individual pursuits, but powerful tools for cultivating the kind of connections that enrich our lives and leave a lasting, positive impact on the world around us. Embrace this journey with an open heart, and witness the profound ways in which self love can transform your relationships and your life.

Chapter 9: Boundaries & Interdependence

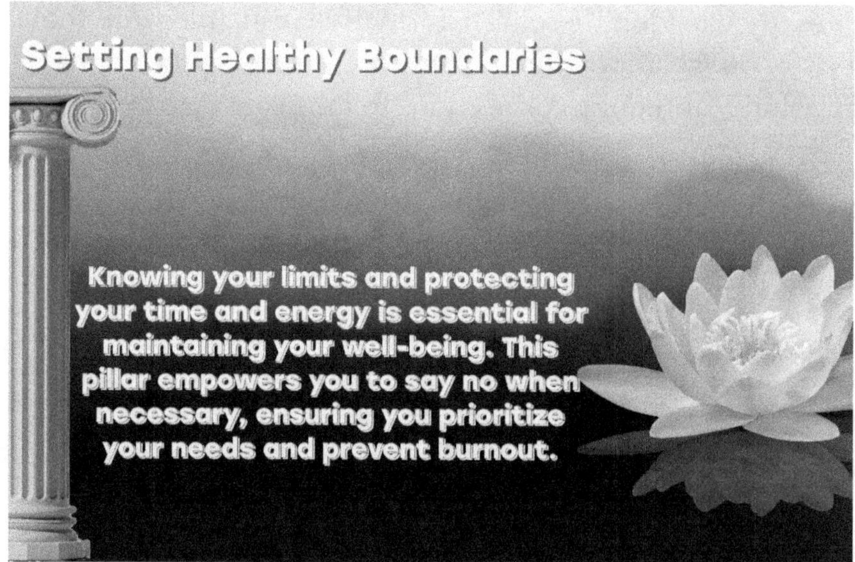

Introduction

As we continue our exploration of self love and healthy relationships, the concepts of boundaries and interdependence take center stage. While establishing boundaries is a crucial component of self care and authenticity, it is equally important to understand how those boundaries can foster deeper, more fulfilling connections with others. This chapter will delve into the delicate balance between honoring our own needs and supporting the needs of those we care about, ultimately leading to a more harmonious and mutually empowering way of relating.

The Power Of Healthy Boundaries

In the previous chapter, we examined the vital role that boundaries play in protecting our emotional, physical, and mental well-being. Boundaries define the limits of what we are willing to accept in our relationships, allowing us to maintain a sense of self and avoid becoming overwhelmed or resentful. When we set clear boundaries, we communicate our needs and values, creating an environment of mutual respect and understanding.

However, the purpose of boundaries extends beyond merely safeguarding our own interests. Healthy boundaries also serve as the foundation for deeper, more fulfilling connections with others. By honoring our limits, we create the space for authentic, balanced relationships to thrive.

Boundaries & Interdependence

Contrary to popular belief, setting boundaries does not inherently lead to isolation or disconnection. In fact, well-defined boundaries can actually enhance our ability to be interdependent – to engage in relationships where we support one another's growth and needs without losing our sense of self.

Interdependence is the recognition that we are all interconnected, and that our well-being is inextricably linked to the well-being of those around us. It is the understanding that we can lean on others for support and nourishment, while still maintaining our own identity and autonomy.

When we establish healthy boundaries, we create the conditions for this interdependence to flourish. By communicating our needs clearly and consistently, we invite our loved ones to respect our limits and engage with us in a way that honors our wholeness. This, in turn, allows us to be more present, vulnerable, and supportive in our relationships, as we no longer feel the need to sacrifice our own needs in order to please others.

The Delicate Balance

Navigating the balance between our own needs and the needs of others can be a delicate dance. It requires a deep understanding of ourselves, as well as a genuine compassion for the experiences and perspectives of those we care about.

On one hand, we must be vigilant in protecting our boundaries, ensuring that we do not become enmeshed or codependent in our relationships. Overextending ourselves or allowing our boundaries to be repeatedly violated can lead to burnout, resentment, and a loss of personal identity.

On the other hand, we must also be willing to show up for our loved ones, to offer support and empathy, and to compromise when appropriate. Rigid boundaries that prevent us from engaging in meaningful, reciprocal relationships can also be detrimental, leading to isolation and a lack of true connection.

The key is to find a harmonious balance – one where we honor our own needs and limits, while also remaining open and responsive to the needs of others. This requires constant self reflection, clear communication, and a willingness to adapt as our circumstances and relationships evolve.

Strategies For Cultivating Healthy Interdependence

Here are some strategies to help you navigate the delicate balance between boundaries and interdependence:

Regular Self Assessment

Periodically check in with yourself to evaluate how well your boundaries are serving you. Are there areas where you feel overextended or resentful? Conversely, are there places where your boundaries may be too rigid, preventing you from fully engaging with your loved ones? Honest self reflection will help you make adjustments as needed.

Communicate Your Needs Clearly & Compassionately

When setting boundaries or negotiating the needs of others, use "I" statements to express your thoughts and feelings. Avoid accusatory language, and instead focus on finding solutions that honor everyone's well-being. Approach these conversations with empathy and a genuine desire to understand the other person's perspective.

Practice Active Listening

When your loved ones share their needs and concerns, make a conscious effort to truly hear and understand them. Paraphrase what they say to confirm your understanding, and ask clarifying questions if needed. This demonstrates that you value their experiences and are committed to finding a mutually satisfactory resolution.

Cultivate Flexibility & Adaptability

Recognize that boundaries and interdependence are not static; they must evolve as our relationships and circumstances change. Be open to revisiting and adjusting your boundaries as needed, and encourage your loved ones to do the same. Flexibility allows you to maintain healthy connections while still honoring your core needs.

Prioritize Self Care

Engaging in consistent self care practices – whether it's meditation, exercise, or simply taking time for yourself – will help you maintain the emotional and mental resources necessary to navigate the complexities of interdependence. When you are well-rested and grounded, you are better equipped to respond to the needs of others without sacrificing your own well-being.

Seek Support & Accountability

Surround yourself with a network of trusted friends, family members, or professionals who can provide guidance and accountability as you explore the balance between boundaries and interdependence. Sharing your experiences and challenges with those who understand can help you gain new perspectives and stay committed to your goals.

Celebrate Small Victories

Acknowledge and appreciate the moments when you successfully navigate the tensions between your needs and the needs of others. Celebrate your growth, your compromises, and your ability to maintain healthy boundaries while deepening your connections. These small wins will reinforce the importance of this delicate balance and inspire you to continue on your journey.

The Path To Harmonious Relationships

Ultimately, the journey of cultivating healthy boundaries and interdependence is an ongoing process, one that requires self awareness, compassion, and a willingness to continuously adapt. By honoring our own needs while also remaining open and responsive to the needs of our loved ones, we create the conditions for truly nourishing, mutually empowering relationships to thrive.

As you navigate this path, remember that there is no one-size-fits-all solution. The balance you strike will be unique to your circumstances and the people in your life. Trust your intuition, communicate with courage and empathy, and be patient with yourself as you explore the boundaries and interdependence that serve you best. In doing so, you will not only enhance your own well-being but also contribute to the creation of a more harmonious, supportive world.

Importance Of Relationship Healthy Boundaries

Establishing and maintaining healthy boundaries is essential for cultivating fulfilling, balanced relationships. Boundaries serve as the invisible lines that define the parameters of our connections, allowing us to engage with others in a way that honors our individual needs and identities. When we prioritize healthy boundaries, we create the foundation for deeper, more authentic intimacy.

Fostering Mutual Respect

Clear boundaries communicate to our partners, friends, and loved ones how we expect to be treated. By expressing our limits and preferences, we invite others to respect our emotional, physical, and personal space. This mutual understanding lays the groundwork for a relationship dynamic built on consideration and care.

Preventing Resentment & Burnout

Without boundaries, we risk becoming resentful and emotionally depleted as we overextend ourselves to meet the demands of others. Healthy boundaries allow us to say "no" when necessary, preserving our energy and emotional resources for the relationships and commitments that truly matter to us. This, in turn, prevents the burnout that can erode the quality of our connections.

Cultivating Autonomy & Interdependence

Paradoxically, boundaries actually enhance our ability to be interdependent within our relationships. When we have a clear sense of our own needs and limits, we are better equipped to show up for our loved ones without losing ourselves in the process. This autonomy allows us to engage in a mutually supportive dynamic, rather than becoming enmeshed or codependent.

Deepening Emotional Intimacy

Vulnerability and authenticity are the hallmarks of truly intimate relationships. However, these qualities can only flourish when we feel safe to express our authentic selves. Boundaries provide that sense of safety, allowing us to open up and share our innermost thoughts and feelings without fear of judgment or rejection.

Modeling Healthy Relational Patterns

The boundaries we establish in our own lives have a profound impact on those around us, especially our children or younger loved ones. When we demonstrate the ability to assert our needs and respect the needs of others, we model healthy relational patterns that can be passed down through generations. This legacy of self care and mutual understanding is an invaluable gift.

Navigating Conflicts Constructively

Inevitably, conflicts will arise within our relationships. However, when we have a foundation of healthy boundaries, we are better equipped to navigate these challenges constructively. We can express our feelings and perspectives clearly, while also making space to hear and understand the viewpoints of our loved ones. This mutual respect fosters resolution rather than escalation.

Ultimately, the importance of healthy boundaries in relationships cannot be overstated. By honoring our own limits and inviting others to do the same, we create the conditions for trust, intimacy, and mutual growth to flourish. Embracing this practice is a profound act of self love that reverberates through all of our connections, transforming the way we relate to ourselves and to the world around us.

Reflective Questions

1. How would you define the relationship between boundaries and interdependence? ____________________________

____

Do you see them as complementary or conflicting concepts?

____

____

2. Reflect on a time when you felt you had struck a healthy balance between your own needs and the needs of someone close to you. What made that situation successful, and how can you apply those lessons to other relationships?

____

____

____

3. Where do you currently struggle the most with balancing your boundaries and your desire to support or connect with others? ______________________________________

____

____

What underlying beliefs or fears might be contributing to this challenge? ___________________________________

____

____

____

4. How do the cultural messages and expectations you've internalized about relationships and self care impact your ability to navigate boundaries and interdependence?

____

____

____

____

How can you challenge these narratives?

____

____

____

____

5. What self care practices or boundary-setting rituals help you feel grounded and centered when navigating the complexities of your relationships? _____________________________

____

____

____

____

How can you make these a more consistent part of your routine? _____________________________

____

____

____

____

____

6. Who in your life models healthy interdependence in a way that inspires you? _______________

____

____

____

What specific qualities or behaviors do you admire, and how can you incorporate them into your own approach?

____

____

____

7. Imagine your ideal state of balance between your boundaries and your connections with others. What does that look like, and what steps can you take to move closer to that vision? _______________

____

____

____

8. How might you involve your loved ones in the process of establishing healthy boundaries and interdependence?

____

____

____

What conversations could you initiate to get them on the same page? _______________

____

____

9. What fears or insecurities come up for you when you think about asserting your boundaries or asking for support from others? ____

____

____

____

How can you approach these challenges with self compassion? ____

____

____

____

10. Looking ahead, what are the most important lessons you want to take away from this exploration of boundaries and interdependence? ____

____

____

____

How will you apply these insights to cultivate more harmonious, fulfilling relationships? ____

____

____

____

Engaging with these reflective questions can help you deepen your understanding of the dynamic interplay between boundaries and interdependence, empowering you to navigate your relationships with greater clarity, empathy, and authenticity.

Chapter Conclusion: Boundaries & Interdependence

As we bring this chapter on boundaries and interdependence to a close, it's clear that this delicate balance is essential for cultivating fulfilling, harmonious relationships. By honoring our own needs and limits, we create the space for deeper, more authentic connections to flourish.

Throughout our exploration, we've seen how healthy boundaries serve as the foundation for true interdependence - the recognition that our well-being is inextricably linked to the well-being of those around us. When we communicate our boundaries clearly and compassionately, we invite our loved ones to engage with us in a way that respects our wholeness. This, in turn, allows us to be more present, vulnerable, and supportive in our relationships, as we no longer feel the need to sacrifice our own needs in order to please others.

However, navigating this balance is not always easy. There is a constant dance between honoring our own limits and responding to the needs of those we care about. It requires ongoing self reflection, flexibility, and a willingness to adapt as our circumstances and relationships evolve.

The strategies we've discussed - from regular self assessment to cultivating adaptability - provide a roadmap for finding this harmonious middle ground. By engaging in these practices, we empower ourselves to set boundaries that protect our well-being without creating unnecessary distance or isolation.

We learn to lean on our support systems, communicate our needs with clarity and empathy, and celebrate the small victories that reinforce the importance of this delicate balance.

Ultimately, the journey of boundaries and interdependence is a lifelong one, with no perfect endpoint. But as we continue to navigate this path with self compassion and a commitment to growth, we open the door to relationships that are truly nourishing - ones where we can show up authentically, offer genuine support, and feel deeply seen and accepted in return.

As you move forward, remember that the boundaries you establish are not barriers, but bridges that allow you to connect more deeply. Trust the wisdom of your intuition, continue to explore your evolving needs, and have the courage to communicate them to those you hold dear. In doing so, you will not only enhance your own well-being, but also contribute to the creation of a more harmonious, mutually empowering world.

Chapter 10: Shared Growth & Mutual Encouragement

Introduction

As we continue our journey of self love and cultivating healthy relationships, the concept of shared growth and mutual encouragement takes center stage. Relationships have the profound potential to be catalysts for personal transformation, when we approach them with a mindset of supporting each other's goals, celebrating each other's wins, and lifting one another up.

In a world that often promotes individualism and competition, the practice of mutual empowerment stands out as a radical act of love and community. By fostering an environment where we champion each other's growth, we not only deepen the intimacy and fulfillment within our connections, but we also contribute to the collective upliftment of those around us.

The Power Of Shared Growth

When we enter relationships with the intention of supporting each other's personal evolution, something magical happens. Our connections become conduits for mutual inspiration, accountability, and empowerment. Rather than seeing our loved ones' progress as a threat to our own, we find joy and pride in witnessing their blossoming.

This dynamic of shared growth nurtures several key benefits:

Deepened Intimacy

As we invest in each other's journeys, we develop a profound understanding and appreciation for the unique paths we each walk. Sharing our dreams, fears, and triumphs creates an unparalleled level of vulnerability and trust, fostering intimacy that transcends the superficial.

Heightened Motivation

The encouragement and celebration we receive from our loved ones can serve as powerful fuel for our own personal growth. Knowing that we have a supportive network cheering us on provides the motivation to keep pushing forward, even in the face of challenges.

Expanded Perspectives

When we open ourselves to the growth of those around us, we simultaneously expand our own horizons. We are exposed to new ideas, approaches, and ways of being that inspire us to explore beyond our familiar boundaries.

Collective Upliftment

Perhaps most importantly, the practice of shared growth creates a ripple effect that extends far beyond our individual relationships. As we lift each other up, we contribute to the collective elevation of our communities and the world at large.

Strategies For Cultivating Mutual Encouragement

So, how do we actively cultivate an environment of shared growth and mutual encouragement within our relationships? Here are some powerful strategies to consider:

Celebrate Each Other's Wins

Make a conscious effort to recognize and celebrate the accomplishments, big and small, of the people in your life. Whether it's a promotion at work, the completion of a personal goal, or simply the courage to try something new, take the time to express genuine excitement and pride. This reinforces the message that you are invested in their success.

Offer Specific Encouragement

Generic words of encouragement can be uplifting, but targeted, personalized support tends to have an even greater impact. Pay attention to the unique challenges and aspirations of your loved ones, and offer encouragement that speaks directly to their individual experiences. This demonstrates that you have truly listened and understand what matters most to them.

Share Resources & Connections

When you come across information, opportunities, or connections that you believe could benefit someone you care about, don't hesitate to share them. This gesture communicates that you are actively looking for ways to support their growth and development. It also helps to expand their network and resources, further fueling their progress.

Hold Space for Vulnerability

Creating an environment where your loved ones feel safe to be vulnerable is crucial for fostering mutual encouragement. Make space for them to share their fears, doubts, and struggles without judgment. Respond with empathy, offering a compassionate ear and perspective rather than unsolicited advice.

Provide Constructive Feedback

While celebration and encouragement are essential, there are times when providing thoughtful, constructive feedback can also serve as a powerful tool for growth. Offer insights that challenge your loved ones to stretch beyond their comfort zones, but do so in a way that is rooted in care and a belief in their potential.

Acknowledge Setbacks With Empathy

Progress is rarely linear, and setbacks are an inevitable part of the growth journey. When your loved ones experience challenges or disappointments, approach them with empathy and compassion. Validate their feelings, and help them reframe the experience as an opportunity to learn and grow, rather than a failure.

Cultivate a Mindset of Abundance

It's all too easy to fall into a scarcity mindset, where we view the success of others as a threat to our own. Consciously shift your perspective to one of abundance, where you recognize that there is ample room for everyone to thrive. This mindset shift allows you to genuinely celebrate the triumphs of those around you.

Lead by Example

Ultimately, the most impactful way to foster a culture of shared growth and mutual encouragement is to embody those values in your own life. Prioritize your personal development, celebrate your own wins, and graciously accept the support and feedback of your loved ones. As you model this behavior, you inspire others to do the same.

Lifting As We Climb

The concept of "lifting as we climb" is a powerful metaphor for the type of relationships we seek to cultivate. It speaks to the idea that as we ascend the mountains of our own personal growth, we extend a hand to those behind us, helping to pull them up as well.

This mindset shift from individualism to collective empowerment is a revolutionary act of love. By championing the success of others, we not only enhance the quality of our own lives, but we also contribute to the betterment of our communities and the world at large.

Imagine a world where we approach our relationships not as zero-sum games, but as collaborative journeys of shared transformation. Where the achievements of our loved ones fill us with genuine pride, rather than envy or resentment. Where we actively seek out ways to support, encourage, and uplift one another, knowing that in doing so, we all rise together.

This is the vision we hold as we continue our exploration of self love and healthy relationships. By cultivating an environment of shared growth and mutual encouragement, we not only deepen the intimacy and fulfillment within our connections, but we also become agents of positive change, inspiring others to do the same.

So, let us embrace this path of collective upliftment, celebrating each other's wins, lifting each other up, and creating a rising tide that carries us all to new heights of personal and relational fulfillment.

Importance Of Shared Growth & Mutual Encouragement In Relationships

Cultivating an environment of shared growth and mutual encouragement within our relationships is not just a nice-to-have; it is an essential element of fostering truly fulfilling, transformative connections. When we approach our loved ones as partners in each other's personal evolution, we unlock a wellspring of benefits that enhance the quality of our lives and the world around us.

Deepened Intimacy

As we invest in each other's journeys, we develop a profound understanding and appreciation for the unique paths we each walk. Sharing our dreams, fears, and triumphs creates an unparalleled level of vulnerability and trust, fostering intimacy that transcends the superficial. This depth of connection allows us to show up for one another in ways that mere surface-level relationships cannot.

Heightened Motivation

The encouragement and celebration we receive from our loved ones can serve as powerful fuel for our own personal growth. Knowing that we have a supportive network cheering us on provides the motivation to keep pushing forward, even in the face of challenges. This mutual accountability and inspiration helps us overcome obstacles and achieve goals we may have once thought unattainable.

Expanded Perspectives

When we open ourselves to the growth of those around us, we simultaneously expand our own horizons. We are exposed to new ideas, approaches, and ways of being that inspire us to explore beyond our familiar boundaries. This cross-pollination of perspectives not only enhances our personal development, but it also equips us to navigate an increasingly complex and diverse world.

Collective Upliftment

Perhaps most importantly, the practice of shared growth creates a ripple effect that extends far beyond our individual relationships. As we lift each other up, we contribute to the collective elevation of our communities and the world at large. This mindset shift from individualism to collaborative empowerment is a revolutionary act of love, one that has the power to transform the human experience.

Cultivating an environment of shared growth and mutual encouragement is not merely a feel-good exercise; it is a strategic investment in the well-being of ourselves, our loved ones, and the greater good. By championing the success of others, we enhance the quality of our own lives while also becoming agents of positive change, inspiring others to do the same.

In a world that often promotes competition and scarcity, this approach to relationships stands out as a radical act of

love and community. It challenges us to reframe our perspectives, to see our connections not as zero-sum games, but as collaborative journeys of shared transformation. And in doing so, we unlock the true power of human potential, both within ourselves and in those we hold dear.

Fostering a Strengths-Based Mindset

When we focus on supporting each other's growth and celebrating each other's wins, we naturally shift away from a deficit-based perspective. Rather than dwelling on weaknesses or shortcomings, we begin to recognize and amplify the unique strengths and talents that each person brings to the table. This strengths-based mindset not only boosts self confidence but also inspires us to leverage our full potential.

Enhancing Resilience

Navigating life's challenges is infinitely easier when we have a network of loved ones who lift us up and provide encouragement. Knowing that we have a safety net of support makes us more willing to take risks, try new things, and bounce back from setbacks. This shared resilience strengthens our ability to weather the storms of life with grace and determination.

Modeling Healthy Relational Patterns

The way we interact with and support our loved ones sets a powerful example, especially for the younger generations. When we demonstrate the ability to champion each other's growth, we model healthy relational patterns that can be passed down through families and communities. This legacy of mutual empowerment has the potential to transform social dynamics and create a more compassionate world.

Combating Isolation & Loneliness

In a society that can often feel disconnected and individualistic, the practice of shared growth and mutual encouragement provides a vital antidote to isolation and loneliness. By fostering an environment where we feel seen, heard, and supported, we cultivate a profound sense of belonging that nourishes our overall well-being.

Increasing Productivity & Innovation

Interestingly, research has shown that when people feel encouraged and empowered by their loved ones, they tend to be more productive, creative, and innovative in their personal and professional pursuits. The positive feedback loop of shared growth fuels our ability to ideate, take risks, and push the boundaries of what we thought possible.

Promoting Healthy Competition

While competition is often framed as a zero-sum game, shared growth and mutual encouragement can actually foster a healthy, collaborative form of competition. When we celebrate each other's successes, we are inspired to raise the bar for ourselves, not out of envy, but out of a genuine desire to grow and excel. This spirit of friendly rivalry can propel us all to new heights.

Enhancing Gratitude&D Generosity

The act of championing each other's growth naturally cultivates a deeper sense of gratitude and a desire to "pay it forward." As we witness the transformative impact of the support and encouragement we receive, we become more inclined to extend that same level of generosity to others. This positive feedback loop creates a culture of abundance and mutual upliftment.

Ultimately, the importance of shared growth and mutual encouragement in relationships cannot be overstated. By approaching our connections as collaborative journeys of transformation, we unlock a wellspring of benefits that enhance not only our individual lives, but the collective human experience. It is a radical act of love that has the power to change the world, one relationship at a time.

So, as we continue our exploration of self love and healthy relationships, let us embrace the transformative potential of shared growth and mutual encouragement. For in lifting each other up, we not only deepen the intimacy and fulfillment within our connections, but we also contribute to the creation of a more harmonious, equitable, and thriving world.

Reflective Questions

1. Reflect on a time when someone in your life actively supported your personal growth and celebrated your achievements. How did that make you feel, and what impact did it have on your journey? _______________________________

____

____

____

____

____

____

____

2. Who in your life do you feel most inspired to support and encourage in their own growth and development?

____

____

____

What specific ways can you demonstrate that support and encouragement? _______________________________

____

____

____

____

3. Where do you tend to fall into a scarcity mindset when it comes to the success of others? ________________________

____

____

____

____

____

What beliefs or fears might be contributing to that perspective, and how can you consciously shift towards an abundance mindset? _______________________________

____

____

____

____

____

____

4. In what areas of your life do you feel you could benefit from more support, accountability, or constructive feedback from your loved ones? ______________________________

____

____

____

How can you communicate those needs effectively?

____

____

____

____

5. Imagine the type of relationships you would like to cultivate, where shared growth and mutual encouragement are the norm. What does that vision look like, and what steps can you take to make it a reality? _______________________

____

____

____

____

____

6. How might prioritizing the growth and success of those around you positively impact your local community or the world at large? _______________________

____

____

____

____

____

What ripple effects can you envision from this collective upliftment? _______________________

____

____

____

____

____

____

7. What are some specific ways you can model the behaviors of shared growth and mutual encouragement in your own life? ____

____

____

How can you make these practices more consistent and intentional? _______________________________________

____

____

8. When you encounter a loved one experiencing a setback or challenge, how can you respond with empathy and help reframe the experience as an opportunity for growth?

____

____

____

____

9. Reflect on your own personal growth journey. In what ways have you been supported and encouraged by others, and how can you pay that forward to someone else?

____

____

____

____

____

10. What fears or doubts come up for you when you consider fully embracing a mindset of collective empowerment?

____

____

____

____

____

____

How can you address those blocks with self compassion and a commitment to your vision?

____

____

____

____

____

____

____

Engaging with these reflective questions can help you deepen your understanding of the power of shared growth and mutual encouragement, and inspire you to cultivate more nourishing, transformative relationships in your life.

Chapter Conclusion: Shared Growth & Mutual Encouragement

As we bring this chapter on shared growth and mutual encouragement to a close, it is clear that this approach to relationships holds the potential to transform not only our individual lives, but the very fabric of our communities and the world at large.

Throughout our exploration, we have witnessed the profound ways in which supporting each other's personal evolution can deepen intimacy, heighten motivation, expand perspectives, and contribute to a collective upliftment. By embracing a mindset of collaborative empowerment, we unlock a wellspring of benefits that nourish the human experience in profound and lasting ways.

The strategies we've discussed - from celebrating each other's wins to cultivating a mindset of abundance - provide a roadmap for bringing this vision to life. They empower us to actively champion the growth and success of our loved ones, recognizing that in doing so, we enhance our own journeys as well.

Ultimately, the practice of shared growth and mutual encouragement is a radical act of love. It challenges us to reframe our relationships, to see them not as zero-sum games, but as collaborative pathways towards collective transformation. It invites us to release the scarcity mindsets and competitive impulses that so often govern our interactions, and instead, to embrace an abundance mentality where there is ample room for everyone to thrive.

As we continue to navigate the complexities of our personal and relational lives, let this chapter serve as a guiding light. Let it inspire us to lift each other up, to celebrate each other's triumphs, and to approach our connections as conduits for mutual inspiration and growth. For in doing so, we not only deepen the intimacy and fulfillment within our own lives, but we also contribute to the creation of a more harmonious, equitable, and thriving world.

Let us embrace this path of shared growth and mutual encouragement, knowing that in lifting each other up, we all rise together. Let us be the change we wish to see, modeling healthy relational patterns that can be passed down through generations. And let us trust that in championing the success of those we hold dear, we unlock the true power of human potential, both within ourselves and in the collective.

The journey ahead may not always be easy, but it is a sacred one - a testament to the transformative power of love, community, and our shared commitment to each other's growth. Let us walk it together, with open hearts, unwavering support, and a deep belief in the boundless possibilities that await us.

Chapter 11: Navigating Conflicts With Self Love

Introduction

Conflict is an inevitable part of any relationship, whether it's with a romantic partner, family member, friend, or colleague. The way we navigate these challenges can make all the difference in the health and longevity of our connections. As we continue our journey of self love and cultivating fulfilling relationships, it's essential to explore how we can approach conflicts from a place of compassion, empathy, and a commitment to resolution.

Far too often, we allow our egos, fears, and unresolved wounds to hijack our responses when faced with disagreements or tensions. We lash out, shut down, or engage in unhealthy patterns that only serve to deepen the divide between us and our loved ones. However, by grounding ourselves in self love and emotional intelligence, we unlock the ability to transform conflicts into opportunities for growth, intimacy, and mutual understanding.

In this chapter, we will delve into practical strategies for managing relational conflicts with self compassion, empathy, and a focus on finding common ground. We'll explore the role of self regulation, effective communication, and a willingness to be vulnerable – all of which are essential for navigating the complexities of human relationships.

The Power Of Self Love In Conflict Resolution

At the heart of our ability to resolve conflicts effectively lies our relationship with ourselves. When we approach disagreements from a place of self love and self acceptance, we are far better equipped to respond with clarity, composure, and a genuine desire for resolution. Self love provides us with several key advantages when navigating conflicts:

Emotional Regulation

By cultivating self love, we enhance our capacity for emotional self regulation. We become better able to identify and manage our own feelings, rather than allowing them to hijack our responses. This emotional intelligence allows us to pause, reflect, and choose how we will engage, rather than reacting impulsively.

Empathy & Compassion

When we love and accept ourselves, we are more likely to extend that same compassion to others. We are better able to see the humanity in those we are in conflict with, recognizing that their own wounds, fears, and perspectives are shaping their behavior. This empathetic stance creates the foundation for mutual understanding.

Resilience & Perseverance

Conflicts can be emotionally taxing, and self love equips us with the resilience to persevere through the challenging moments. We are less likely to become discouraged or give up when faced with disagreements, knowing that our self worth is not contingent on the outcome. This perseverance allows us to navigate conflicts with patience and a commitment to resolution.

Authenticity & Vulnerability

Self love fosters the courage to be authentic and vulnerable in our relationships. When we feel secure in who we are, we are more willing to take emotional risks, share our true feelings, and listen openly to the perspectives of others. This vulnerability is essential for building trust and finding common ground.

Healthy Boundaries

Conflicts often arise when our boundaries have been crossed or when we are unsure of how to assert our needs. Self love gives us the clarity and confidence to set healthy boundaries, communicate them effectively, and hold space for our own and others' limits.

By grounding ourselves in self love, we create the conditions for conflicts to become opportunities for deeper connection, mutual understanding, and personal growth. Rather than seeing disagreements as threats to our relationships, we can approach them as invitations to strengthen the bonds we share.

Strategies For Navigating Conflicts With Self Love

With self love as our foundation, let's explore practical strategies for navigating conflicts in a way that honors our own needs and the needs of our loved ones:

Practice Self Awareness & Emotional Intelligence

Before engaging in a conflict, take time to tune into your internal landscape. Identify the emotions you are experiencing, the thoughts that are driving those feelings, and any unresolved wounds or triggers that may be influencing your perspective. This self awareness allows you to approach the situation with clarity and intentionality.

Communicate With Clarity & Compassion

When expressing your concerns or needs, use "I" statements to convey your perspective without placing blame. Speak from a place of vulnerability, acknowledging your own role in the conflict and your desire to find a resolution. Simultaneously, make a conscious effort to truly listen to the other person, seeking to understand their point of view with empathy and an open mind.

Regulate Your Emotional Responses

When tensions rise, it can be all too easy to get swept up in reactive behaviors like yelling, stonewalling, or passive aggression. Instead, pause, take a few deep breaths, and consciously choose how you will respond. Remind yourself of your commitment to self love and constructive conflict resolution.

Focus On Solutions, Not Blame

When conflicts arise, it's easy to get caught up in pointing fingers and assigning fault. Instead, shift your mindset to one of problem-solving. Collaborate with the other person to brainstorm potential solutions, compromises, or ways to move forward in a manner that honors both of your needs.

Seek To Understand, Not Just To Be Understood

Resist the urge to solely focus on getting your own needs met. Make a genuine effort to understand the other person's perspective, their underlying motivations, and the root causes of the conflict. This curiosity and willingness to see things from their vantage point creates the foundation for mutual understanding.

Embrace Vulnerability & Humility

Be willing to admit when you are wrong, to apologize sincerely, and to acknowledge your own role in the conflict. This vulnerability and humility not only models healthy behavior but also creates the space for the other person to do the same. It facilitates the rebuilding of trust and paves the way for deeper connection.

Prioritize Empathy & Validation

Make a conscious effort to validate the other person's feelings and experiences, even if you don't fully agree with their perspective. Seek to understand where they are coming from, and communicate that you hear and respect their point of view. This empathetic stance can diffuse tensions and open the door for productive dialogue.

Setting & Enforcing Boundaries

If the conflict escalates to the point where your own needs or safety are being compromised, be willing to set clear boundaries and enforce them. This may involve taking a break from the conversation, removing yourself from the situation, or communicating consequences if disrespectful behavior continues. Maintaining healthy boundaries is an act of self love.

Seek External Support if Needed

In some cases, particularly for long-standing or deeply entrenched conflicts, it may be helpful to enlist the support of a neutral third party, such as a therapist, mediator, or trusted mutual friend. This outside perspective can provide valuable insights and facilitate a constructive resolution.

Reflect, Learn, & Grow

After the conflict has been resolved (or at least temporarily addressed), take time to reflect on the experience. Identify the lessons you have learned, the areas where you can improve your conflict resolution skills, and any unresolved emotional wounds that may have contributed to the dynamic. This self reflection will inform your approach to future conflicts.

Navigating Conflicts With Self Love: A Transformative Journey

Approaching conflicts from a place of self love is not always easy, especially when our emotions are running high and our deepest fears and insecurities are triggered. However, it is a profoundly transformative practice that has the power to not only strengthen our relationships but also deepen our own self understanding and personal growth.

When we bring self compassion, emotional intelligence, and a genuine desire for resolution to our conflicts, we create the conditions for true intimacy to flourish. We move beyond the superficial battles of "winning" or "losing" and instead focus on the shared goal of finding common ground and nourishing the connection we share.

This journey of navigating conflicts with self love is an ongoing process, one that requires patience, practice, and a willingness to be vulnerable. There will be times when we stumble, when our own wounds or fears get the better of us. But by returning to the foundation of self love, we can always find our way back to a place of clarity, empathy, and a commitment to resolution.

As we continue to cultivate this approach to conflict, we not only enhance the quality of our relationships but also contribute to the creation of a more harmonious world. We model healthy, constructive ways of engaging with differences, inspiring those around us to do the same.

In this way, our personal journeys of self love and conflict resolution have the power to ripple outward, creating positive change that extends far beyond our individual lives.

So, let us embrace this path of navigating conflicts with self love, knowing that in doing so, we unlock new depths of connection, understanding, and personal growth. Let us be the change we wish to see, one disagreement at a time, and trust that in honoring ourselves and our loved ones, we will find the keys to unlocking a more peaceful, fulfilling, and joyful way of relating.

Importance Of Navigating Conflicts With Self Love

Navigating conflicts and disagreements in our relationships is an inevitable part of the human experience. However, the way we approach these challenges can have a profound impact on the health, longevity, and depth of our connections.

By grounding ourselves in self love and emotional intelligence, we unlock a wellspring of benefits that not only enhance our personal growth but also contribute to the creation of more harmonious, fulfilling relationships.

Enhanced Emotional Regulation

When we approach conflicts from a place of self love, we strengthen our capacity for emotional self regulation. Rather than allowing our feelings to hijack our responses, we become better able to pause, reflect, and choose how we will engage. This emotional intelligence allows us to communicate our needs and perspectives clearly, while also making space to truly listen to the other person.

Increased Empathy & Compassion

Self love fosters the ability to extend compassion not just to ourselves, but also to those we are in conflict with. By recognizing our shared humanity and the unique perspectives and wounds that shape each person's behavior, we cultivate a stance of empathy. This empathetic understanding creates the foundation for mutual understanding and a genuine desire to find common ground.

Greater Resilience & Perseverance

Conflicts can be emotionally taxing, and self love equips us with the resilience to persevere through the challenging moments. We are less likely to become discouraged or give up when faced with disagreements, knowing that our self worth is not contingent on the outcome. This perseverance allows us to navigate conflicts with patience and a commitment to resolution.

Deeper Authenticity & Vulnerability

When we feel secure in our self love, we are more willing to take emotional risks, share our true feelings, and listen openly to the perspectives of others. This vulnerability is essential for building trust and finding common ground. By embracing authenticity, we create the conditions for our relationships to deepen and evolve in meaningful ways.

Clearer Boundaries & Assertiveness

Conflicts often arise when our boundaries have been crossed or when we are unsure of how to assert our needs. Self love gives us the clarity and confidence to set healthy boundaries, communicate them effectively, and hold space for our own and others' limits. This, in turn, fosters mutual respect and a more balanced dynamic within our relationships.

Healthier Communication Patterns

By approaching conflicts with self love, we are better equipped to communicate in a clear, compassionate, and constructive manner. We shift away from reactive behaviors like yelling or stonewalling, and instead focus on expressing our needs, validating the other person's experiences, and collaborating to find solutions. This healthy communication lays the groundwork for more fulfilling, long-lasting connections.

Collective Ripple Effect

When we navigate conflicts with self love, we not only enhance the quality of our own relationships but also contribute to the creation of a more harmonious world. By modeling healthy, constructive ways of engaging with differences, we inspire those around us to do the same. In this way, our personal journeys of self love and conflict resolution have the power to create positive change that extends far beyond our individual lives.

Deeper Intimacy & Trust

When we approach conflicts with self love, we create the conditions for true intimacy and trust to flourish in our relationships. By being vulnerable, validating each other's experiences, and focusing on finding common ground, we build a foundation of mutual understanding that transcends the surface-level disagreements. This depth of connection strengthens the bonds we share and makes our relationships more resilient.

Enhanced Personal Growth

Conflicts, when navigated skillfully, can serve as powerful catalysts for personal growth and self discovery. By reflecting on our role in the conflict, identifying our triggers and patterns, and consciously choosing to respond with self love, we gain invaluable insights about ourselves. This self awareness equips us to make more conscious choices, strengthen our emotional intelligence, and

continue evolving as individuals.

Healthier Conflict Resolution Modeling

The way we handle conflicts sets a powerful example, especially for the younger generations in our lives. When we demonstrate the ability to navigate disagreements with compassion, empathy, and a commitment to resolution, we model healthy relational patterns that can be passed down through families and communities. This legacy of constructive conflict resolution has the potential to transform social dynamics and create a more peaceful, understanding world.

Reduced Stress & Anxiety

Unresolved or poorly managed conflicts can be a major source of stress and anxiety, both within the relationship and for the individuals involved. By approaching these challenges with self love and effective strategies, we mitigate the negative physiological and psychological impacts. This, in turn, enhances our overall well-being and allows us to show up more fully in all aspects of our lives.

Increased Productivity & Creativity

Interestingly, research has shown that when people feel emotionally supported and empowered by their loved ones, they tend to be more productive, creative, and innovative in their personal and professional pursuits. The positive feedback loop of navigating conflicts with self love fuels our ability to ideate, take risks, and push the boundaries of what we thought possible.

Cultivation of Gratitude & Generosity

The act of approaching conflicts with compassion and a genuine desire for resolution naturally cultivates a deeper sense of gratitude and a willingness to "pay it forward." As we witness the transformative impact of self love in our relationships, we become more inclined to extend that same level of generosity to others. This positive feedback loop creates a culture of abundance, understanding, and mutual upliftment.

Contribution to Collective Healing

When we navigate conflicts with self love, we don't just enhance our individual relationships; we also contribute to the collective healing and transformation of our communities and society as a whole. By modeling healthy, constructive ways of engaging with differences, we inspire others to do the same, slowly but surely shifting the dominant paradigm away from divisiveness and towards greater unity.

Ultimately, the importance of navigating conflicts with self love cannot be overstated. It is a revolutionary act of love that has the power to change the world, one relationship at a time. By embracing this approach, we unlock a wellspring of benefits that not only enrich our personal lives but also contribute to the creation of a more harmonious, fulfilling, and joyful human experience.

Reflective Questions

1. Reflect on a time when you navigated a conflict in a way
that honored your self love and emotional intelligence. What
strategies did you employ, and how did that approach impact
the outcome? ____

____

____

____

____

____

2. Where do you tend to struggle the most when it comes to
managing conflicts in your relationships? ___________________

____

____

____

____

What underlying fears, triggers, or unresolved wounds might
be contributing to those challenges? _______________________

____

____

____

____

____

3. How does your current approach to conflicts align with or differ from the strategies outlined in this chapter?

____

____

What insights or "aha moments" emerged as you read through the techniques for navigating conflicts with self love?

____

____

____

4. Imagine a conflict you are currently facing or anticipate facing in the near future. How might you apply the principles of self love, emotional regulation, and constructive communication to that situation? Visualize the potential outcome. ____

____

____

____

5. Who in your life models healthy, self loving conflict resolution in a way that inspires you?

____

____

What specific qualities or behaviors do you admire, and how can you incorporate them into your own approach?

____

____

6. In what ways has your cultural or familial background shaped your beliefs and behaviors around conflicts?

____

____

How can you consciously challenge any unhealthy patterns you've inherited and align your actions with self love?

____

____

7. What fears or insecurities come up for you when you think about being vulnerable, expressing your needs, or compromising during a conflict?

____

____

____

How can you approach these challenges with self compassion?

____

____

____

8. Reflect on a time when you responded to a conflict in a way that you later regretted. What did you learn from that experience, and how can you apply those lessons to future challenges?

____

____

____

9. How might involving your loved ones in the process of navigating conflicts with self love impact the quality and depth of your relationships?

____

____

What conversations could you initiate to get them on the same page? _______________________________________

____

____

10. Looking ahead, what are the most important takeaways you want to carry forward from this exploration of navigating conflicts with self love?

____

____

____

How will you integrate these insights into your daily life and relationships? ________________________________

____

____

____

Engaging with these reflective questions can help you deepen your understanding of the role of self love in conflict resolution, empower you to approach future challenges with clarity and compassion, and contribute to the creation of more harmonious, fulfilling relationships.

Conclusion : Navigating Conflicts With Self Love

The Chapter, Navigating Conflicts with Self love emphasizes the significance of self love in managing conflicts within relationships. It opens by recognizing that conflict is an unavoidable aspect of human connections, and how we handle these situations can greatly affect the strength and longevity of our relationships. The chapter posits that when we allow our egos and unresolved issues to dictate our responses, we often engage in destructive patterns. However, grounding ourselves in self love enables us to transform conflicts into opportunities for growth, intimacy, and understanding.

The chapter outlines several benefits of self love in conflict resolution, including enhanced emotional regulation, increased empathy, resilience, authenticity, and the establishment of healthy boundaries. It advocates for practical strategies that promote self awareness, effective communication, emotional regulation, and a focus on solutions rather than blame. The importance of vulnerability, humility, and seeking to understand others is also highlighted as essential for fostering deeper connections.

Additionally, the chapter discusses the collective impact of navigating conflicts with self love, suggesting that such practices not only enhance personal relationships but also contribute to societal healing and unity. It concludes by encouraging readers to reflect on their conflict resolution experiences, identify areas for improvement, and integrate self love principles into their daily interactions.

Overall, the chapter, Navigating Conflicts with Self love serves as a guide for embracing self love as a transformative force in resolving conflicts, ultimately leading to healthier, more fulfilling relationships and personal growth.

Chapter 12: Self Love, Part 6, Nurturing Inner Beauty and Embracing Self Care

Introduction

Self Love, Part 6, Nurturing Inner Beauty and Embracing Self Care invites you to embark on a transformative journey that underscores the importance of self care as a vital practice for nurturing both inner beauty and overall well-being. This section emphasizes that self care is not merely a luxury but an essential commitment to honoring our needs and enhancing our self worth.

Embracing Self Care

In this chapter, you are introduced to the essence of self care, which is framed as a holistic approach that nurtures physical, emotional, mental, and spiritual health. This mindset encourages you to cultivate self compassion and embrace your unique qualities, reinforcing the idea that everyone is deserving of love and kindness—especially from themselves.

Key Highlights

The Essence of Self Care

Self care is presented as a mindset and commitment to recognizing our inherent worth. It encourages self compassion and the acceptance of our imperfections, allowing us to honor our well-being.

Practical Self Care Techniques

The chapter provides a variety of practical techniques to incorporate self care into daily routines. These include mindfulness meditation, journaling, engaging in physical activity, nurturing creativity, and connecting with nature. Each of these practices is designed to enhance inner beauty and foster a deeper sense of self awareness.

Understanding Inner Beauty

Inner beauty is highlighted as a reflection of our character and values, shaped by how we treat ourselves and others. Cultivating self acceptance and self compassion are emphasized as foundational elements in nurturing this beauty.

Building a Personalized Self Care Routine

You are encouraged to create a self care routine tailored to your unique needs and preferences. This personalized approach ensures that self care becomes a sustainable and integral part of your life.

The Power of Community Support

The chapter emphasizes the importance of engaging with supportive relationships and community groups. Sharing experiences and encouraging one another to prioritize self care can significantly enhance individual journeys.

Conclusion: Embrace Your Self Care Journey

As you conclude this chapter, remember that embracing self care is a vital commitment to nurturing your inner beauty and overall well-being. By integrating self care practices into your daily life, you embark on a lifelong journey of self discovery, growth, and empowerment.

Prioritizing self care not only enhances your confidence and radiance but also creates a ripple effect, inspiring those around you to embrace their own journeys of Self Love. Embrace this transformative journey with open arms, knowing that you are worthy of the love and care you give to yourself.

Don't miss the chance to explore Self Love, Part 6, Nurturing Inner Beauty, Embracing Self Care. This chapter is a treasure trove of insights and practical strategies that will empower you to nurture your inner beauty and cultivate a fulfilling, balanced life. Start your self care journey today, and watch as your confidence and radiance flourish!

Your Path Forward

As you continue your journey through the series, embrace each part, each book, as a stepping stone towards greater self awareness and personal growth. The time to love yourself is now—take that first step with Self Love, Part 1, Understanding Self Love, continue with Self Love, Part 2, The Journey Within, and Self Love, Part 3, Practicing Self Love, Self Love, Part 4, Overcoming Obstacles, Self Love, Part 5, Living a Life of Self Love and conclude with Self Love, Part 6, Nurturing Inner Beauty and Embracing Self, and watch how it transforms your world, guiding you towards a life of authenticity, purpose, and profound self acceptance.

Read Self Love, Part 7, The Freedom of Healthy Boundaries, anytime after you feel you have a positive understanding of Self Love, Part 1, Understanding Self Love.

Reading through the entire series will provide you with a comprehensive roadmap to self love and well-being, empowering you to thrive despite the challenges you face. Let this journey be your guide to a life filled with love, joy, and renewal.

Watch how this book series and your work transforms your world, guiding you towards a life of authenticity, purpose, and profound self acceptance.

Let this journey be your guide to a life filled with love, joy, and renewal!

Chapter 13: Self Love, Part 7, The Freedom Of Healthy Boundaries

Introduction

In "Self Love, Part 7, The Freedom of Healthy Boundaries," you are guided through the essential concept of establishing and maintaining healthy boundaries as a vital aspect of self love and personal empowerment.

This section emphasizes that boundaries are not barriers that isolate us, but rather protective measures that foster emotional well-being and strengthen relationships.

You will learn how to identify your personal limits, communicate them effectively, and uphold them with confidence. By doing so, you can create a safe environment that nurtures your mental and emotional health, allowing you to thrive authentically.

Key Highlights

Understanding Boundaries

Clarifies the definition of healthy boundaries and their importance in maintaining emotional and physical well-being.

Impact of Healthy Boundaries

Discusses the positive effects of setting boundaries on self esteem, relationships, and overall mental health.

Types of Boundaries

Explores various types of boundaries—emotional, physical, digital, and relational—and how each serves a unique purpose in personal interactions.

Communicating Boundaries Effectively

Provides practical strategies for expressing boundaries assertively and respectfully, minimizing misunderstandings in relationships.

Identifying Personal Limits

Guides readers in recognizing their own needs and limits, empowering them to articulate their boundaries clearly.

Coping With Resistance

Offers insights on how to handle pushback or resistance from others when enforcing personal boundaries, emphasizing the importance of self advocacy.

Boundary Maintenance

Encourages readers to regularly assess and adjust their boundaries as needed, recognizing that personal growth may require evolving limits.

Overcoming Guilt

Addresses the common feelings of guilt that can arise when setting boundaries and teaches readers how to overcome these emotions through self affirmation.

The Ripple Effect

Illustrates how establishing healthy boundaries not only benefits the individual but also positively impacts their relationships and communities, creating a culture of respect and understanding.

Empowerment Through Boundaries

Reinforces the idea that healthy boundaries empower individuals to take charge of their lives, fostering a sense of freedom and authenticity in their interactions.

By focusing on the freedom that comes from establishing healthy boundaries, this section equips readers with the tools and confidence needed to protect their well-being and cultivate meaningful connections, ultimately enhancing their journey toward self love and acceptance.

Conclusion

As we reach the end of this transformative journey together, take a moment to reflect on the profound path you have undertaken. In Self Love, Part 3, Practicing Self Love, you have delved into the essence of self connection through daily rituals, explored the power of affirmations, and understood the vital connection between caring for your mind and body. You have also learned the importance of setting healthy boundaries, embraced creative expression as a form of self love, and reconnected with nature to nurture your spirit.

Celebrate the progress you have made throughout this exploration. Recognize the courage it took to establish mindful morning and evening routines, the insights gained from crafting personalized affirmations, and the commitment to maintaining a balanced lifestyle that nurtures both your mind and body.

Each step you've taken—whether it was setting boundaries, engaging in creative pursuits, or finding solace in nature—has contributed to your growth and deepened your understanding of self love. These milestones, no matter how small, represent significant achievements on your path to self acceptance and inner peace.

Your Path Forward

As you look forward, remember that self love is not a destination but a lifelong practice. It requires ongoing reflection, adaptation, and growth. Embrace the understanding that you are constantly evolving, and your practices may shift as you navigate new experiences and challenges in life. This dynamic nature of self love invites you to remain open to learning and developing, encouraging you to revisit and refine your daily rituals, affirmations, and self care practices regularly.

Continuous growth is vital for nurturing self love. As you move forward, consider integrating daily practices that reinforce your commitment to yourself. This could involve setting aside time for self reflection, engaging in activities that bring you joy, or surrounding yourself with supportive individuals who uplift and inspire you. By incorporating these practices into your life, you will not only enhance your self love journey but also create a ripple effect, positively impacting those around you.

When you embrace and embody self love, you inspire others to do the same, fostering a culture of compassion and authenticity in your relationships and communities. As you close this chapter, carry with you the insights and tools you have gained. Trust in your ability to navigate life with self love as your guiding principle. Embrace the journey ahead with an open heart and mind, knowing that self love is an evolving practice that enriches your life and the lives of those around you. You are worthy of love, growth, and fulfillment—now and always.

Chapter 14: Conclusion

As we reach the end of this journey together, take a moment to reflect on the transformative path you have undertaken. You have ventured into the depths of Self discovery, explored your core values, and crafted actionable plans to align your life with what truly matters to you. This process has not only deepened your Self Awareness but has also laid the groundwork for cultivating a profound sense of Self Love.

It is essential to celebrate the progress you have made throughout this exploration. Recognize the courage it took to confront your beliefs, the insights you gained about yourself, and the commitment to living authentically. Each step you've taken—whether it was identifying influential moments, creating a values list, or actively embodying your chosen values—has contributed to your growth and understanding of yourself. Celebrate these milestones, no matter how small, as they represent significant achievements in your journey toward Self Love.

As you look forward, remember that Self Love is not a destination but a lifelong practice. It requires ongoing reflection, adaptation, and growth. Embrace the understanding that you are constantly evolving, and your values may shift as you navigate new experiences and challenges in life. This dynamic nature of Self Love invites you to remain open to learning and developing, encouraging you to revisit your values and action plans regularly.

Continuous growth is vital for nurturing Self Love. As you move forward, consider integrating daily practices that reinforce your commitment to yourself. This could involve setting aside time for Self Reflection, engaging in activities that bring you joy, or surrounding yourself with supportive individuals who uplift and inspire you.

Incorporating these practices into your life will not only enhance your Self Love journey but also create a ripple effect, positively impacting those around you. When you embrace and embody Self Love, you inspire others to do the same, fostering a culture of compassion and authenticity in your relationships and communities.

As you close this chapter, carry with you the insights and tools you have gained. Trust in your ability to navigate life with your core values as your compass. Embrace the journey ahead with an open heart and mind, knowing that Self Love is an evolving practice that enriches your life and the lives of those around you. You are worthy of love, growth, and fulfillment—now and always.

Appendices: Key Concepts

Authenticity

The quality of being true to oneself, expressing genuine thoughts, feelings, and values without pretense or conformity to external expectations.

Empowerment

The process of gaining confidence and control over one's life, enabling individuals to make choices that align with their true selves.

Awakening

A journey of self discovery and heightened awareness, leading to personal growth and a deeper understanding of one's true identity.

Inner Critic

The negative self talk or critical voice within that can undermine self esteem and hinder the acceptance of one's true self.

Connection

The relationships and bonds we form with others; embracing authenticity can lead to deeper, more meaningful connections.

Mindfulness

The practice of being present and fully engaged in the moment, which helps individuals become more aware of their thoughts and emotions, facilitating authenticity.

Personal Growth

The ongoing process of self improvement and development in various aspects of life, including emotional, spiritual, and intellectual dimensions.

Self Love

The practice of valuing and caring for oneself, involving self acceptance and prioritizing personal well-being.

Vulnerability

The willingness to show one's true self, including emotions and imperfections, which fosters deeper connections with others.

Resilience

The ability to bounce back from challenges and adversity, fostering strength and a positive mindset in the pursuit of authenticity.

Self Acceptance

The recognition and acceptance of one's own thoughts, feelings, and characteristics, leading to a more compassionate relationship with oneself.

Appendices: Recommended Readings, Podcasts, & Websites

To further enrich your journey toward self love and acceptance, consider exploring the following resources that align with the themes of self advocacy, assertive communication, and personal empowerment:

Books

"The Gifts of Imperfection" by Brené Brown: A powerful exploration of embracing imperfections and cultivating self compassion, setting a foundation for self advocacy.

"You Are a Badass" by Jen Sincero: A motivational guide that encourages self acceptance and living boldly, perfect for those looking to enhance their self advocacy skills.

"Radical Acceptance" by Tara Brach: This transformative read emphasizes embracing ourselves and our lives with compassion and mindfulness, key elements in advocating for one's needs.

"The Self Love Experiment" by Shannon Kaiser: A practical guide filled with actionable steps and personal anecdotes to help you cultivate self love through effective self advocacy practices.

"Boundaries: When to Say Yes, How to Say No" by Dr. Henry Cloud and Dr. John Townsend: This book offers insights into setting and maintaining healthy boundaries, essential for self advocacy and interdependent relationships.

Podcasts

"The Self Love Podcast" with Jessica Ortner: Engaging conversations focused on self love practices, including tips and interviews with experts in the field.

"Unlocking Us" with Brené Brown: A podcast exploring vulnerability, courage, and the importance of self acceptance, which can greatly enhance your self advocacy journey.

"The Mindful Kind" with Rachael O'Meara: Insights on mindfulness and self compassion to enhance your daily life and support your self advocacy efforts.

"Therapy Chat": This podcast delves into themes of self advocacy, mental health, and personal growth, providing valuable insights for navigating relationships.

Websites

Self Love Project: A resource hub offering articles, exercises, and community support focused on self love and personal growth, with a strong emphasis on self advocacy.

Tiny Buddha: A website dedicated to mindfulness, self acceptance, and well-being, featuring articles, quotes, and community discussions that inspire self advocacy.

Mindful.org: A platform promoting mindfulness practices, offering resources and tools to help you cultivate self awareness and self love.

The Gottman Institute: This resource offers insights into building healthy relationships, enhancing communication skills, and advocating for your needs within various types of relationships.

As you engage with these readings, podcasts, and websites, remember that the journey to self love and self advocacy is continuous. Use these tools to guide you, inspire you, and reinforce your commitment to living authentically and embracing your true self. Your journey is unique, and with each step you take, you are creating a fulfilling life rooted in love, acceptance, and growth.

About The Author

Lady Kimberly Motes Doty

Lady Kimberly Motes Doty is a beacon of inspiration and empowerment, touching lives around the globe as an internationally acclaimed author, spiritual life coach, and wellness expert. With a heart full of compassion and a spirit driven by faith, she dedicates her life to uplifting others and guiding them on their unique journeys toward self discovery and fulfillment.

A multifaceted woman, Lady Kimberly's diverse background spans technology, health, and holistic wellness. Her impressive credentials include certifications as a Certified Natural Health Professional, Life Coach, Spirituality Coach, and Professional Body Healing Coach. These qualifications, coupled with her rich academic achievements—a Master of Science in Business, a Bachelor of Science in Computer Science, and an Associate of Applied Science in Computer Information Management Systems

—equip her to offer profound insights into the complexities of personal growth and well-being.

As a bestselling author, Lady Kimberly has penned transformative works that resonate with readers of all ages. Her globally bestselling book in the Inspirational category, along with her acclaimed children's series "Discovering God's Love," weaves valuable lessons into engaging narratives. The "Empowered Vibrant Living" series serves as a roadmap for those seeking to embrace healthier lifestyles, while her "Soul Reflections" and "The Whimsical World of the Littles" series infuse messages of self acceptance, faith, and personal growth into the hearts of readers.

More than just a writer, Lady Kimberly is a devoted mother, grandmother, and wife. Her roles as a nurturing figure and a pillar of strength in her family enrich her perspective, enabling her to connect deeply with others. Through her lived experiences, she exemplifies the power of resilience and the importance of nurturing one's spirit.

Lady Kimberly's commitment to holistic well-being and self love inspires countless individuals to reclaim their personal power and live with purpose. With every book she writes and every heart she touches, she fosters a community rooted in authenticity, compassion, and joy.

Join Lady Kimberly on her journey of empowerment and transformation. Discover the profound insights within her books and allow her words to guide you toward a life filled with love, acceptance, and vibrant living. Embrace the gift of self discovery and let your own light shine brightly!.

Book Summary

Dive into a transformative journey with Self Love, Part 5, Embracing Authenticity: A Journey of Self Discovery and Connection from the acclaimed A Godly Life series by Lady Kimberly Motes Doty. This enlightening volume invites readers to explore the depths of self love and authenticity, providing the tools and insights needed to cultivate genuine connections with oneself and others.

Whether you're struggling with self worth, seeking deeper connections, or simply yearning for personal growth, this book offers a roadmap to living with intention, joy, and authenticity.

Unlock Your True Self and Transform Your Relationships!

In Self Love, Part 5, Embracing Authenticity of the A Godly Life series, Lady Kimberly Motes Doty invites you on an empowering journey toward self discovery and genuine connection. As the world bombards us with unrealistic expectations and pressures to conform, this enlightening guide encourages you to break free from self doubt and embrace the unique beauty of who you truly are.

Delve into the heart of self love and uncover the core values that define you. Through personal stories, reflective exercises, and practical tools, you will learn to cultivate authentic relationships built on mutual respect, empathy, and understanding.

Inside, you will discover:

- ▸ The Power of Core Values: Identify and embrace the guiding principles that shape your life and decisions.

- ▸ Transformative Practices: Integrate daily rituals, intentional prayers, and meditation techniques into your routine.

- ▸ -Navigating Relationships: Enhance your connections with others by practicing self love, setting healthy boundaries, and fostering mutual encouragement.

- ▸ Overcoming Challenges: Gain strategies to conquer self doubt and fear, empowering you to advocate for your needs confidently.

Self Love, Part 5, Embracing Authenticity